Fisherman's Winter

RODERICK HAIG-BROWN

Fisherman's Winter

Illustrated by Louis Darling

 LYONS & BURFORD, PUBLISHERS

PRINTED IN THE UNITED STATES OF AMERICA

10   9   8   7   6   5   4   3   2

LIBRARY OF CONGRESS CATALOGING-IN PUBLICATION DATA

HAIG-BROWN, RODERICK LANGMERE, 1908-1976.
   FISHERMAN'S WINTER.

   REPRINT. ORIGINALLY PUBLISHED: NEW YORK:
MORROW, 1954.
   1. FISHING—CHILE. 2. FISHING—ARGENTINA.
3. TROUT FISHING—SOUTH AMERICA. I. TITLE.
SH587.H34   1988   799.1'1'0983   88-8246
ISBN 1-55821-015-6

Contents

APPENDICES

Preface to the 1975 Edition

When *Fisherman's Winter* was first published, some of my friends were disappointed that I had written it about South America rather than about the winter steelhead streams of the Pacific Northwest. It would have been more in keeping with the rest of the series to have kept to North America and written of a real winter instead of a second summer, but at the time I was so excited about the rivers and the fishing I had found in South America that I couldn't wait to write about them. Perhaps I may still find time and inclination to write of a North American fishing winter, though aging bones are more likely to seek the fireside than the cold and stress of winter-flowing streams.

When I went to Chile and Argentina more than twenty years ago I was told repeatedly, "Of course, the fishing is not what it was." Perhaps not, but it was still wonderfully good. I am told today by people who have fished recently in South America, "Of course, it isn't the way it was when you were there." Perhaps not; nowhere in the world is the fishing as good as it was in the memories of the oldtimers, and I sometimes suspect it never was quite that good. But it remains pretty good in many places, and I am sure Chile and Argentina are no exception to this. My friend Lee Richardson, who has returned several times since 1952, has managed to find good fish in most of the streams. Friends write or visit from time to time to tell me it is not what it was, then contradict themselves with stories of good days and fine fish.

Several of the famous streams, like Trancura and Liucura and Tolten, Fui, Enco, and San Pedro have been damaged by volcanic eruptions but have recovered extremely well. The Laja was damaged by heavy floods a few years ago but already is providing fish of three, four, and five pounds. I hear rather less frequently of the Argentine pampas streams, but should be very surprised if rivers like the Malleo, Chimehuin, and Collon Cura are not providing fish as well as ever, and their sparkling beauty is not likely to have faded.

Several fishermen I know have now found their way down to Patagonia and Tierra del Fuego. I understand it is a place of big fish and awful weather. There have been more disappointments than successes, more tales of being blown off the water than of big fish beached. But fishermen are never easily discouraged by wind or weather and no doubt will bravely face all the winds of Cape Horn if there is a twenty-pound trout to be found somewhere.

It is impossible not to feel sadness for the political tribulations of both Argentine and Chile. The Chileans especially are such happy people, so proud of their country, its democratic traditions, and their own good nature that any thought of their distress is overwhelming. No doubt they rise above it and welcome the stranger as they always have, with companionship, good humor, and easy laughter. I hope one day to run a Chilean river again and stop at noon to drink a bottle of good Chilean wine through the mythical *mala hora.*

Roderick Haig-Brown
April 1975

Flight

NORMALLY I AM A STAY-AT-HOME fisherman, no great organizer of expeditions to far fields and fresh streams. I enjoy my fishing as a byproduct of daily life and I enjoy above all things the familiar challenges of a well-known stream. I have, of course, taken the reasonable precaution of living most of my life within easy reach of good trout and salmon streams, but that has been no great hardship. Good trout streams and good country are likely to go together.

When I first planned this book I expected to write in it of my own familiar British Columbia waters, with perhaps a word or two about winter fishing in other places where chance has taken me. But in the winter of 1951-52 I was asked to go south to investigate the trout fishing of Chile and Argentina. It was the sort of assignment that any fisherman might be allowed to dream about in his more wildly optimistic moments, but certainly not one that a reasonably cautious man would expect to have offered to him as a sudden, tangible reality. I was cautious enough to ask a few questions, but only a few. The job, it seemed, was to investigate the fishing thoroughly, with special attention to fly fishing, accessibility, accommodations and other factors bearing upon the comfort of the fisherman; to be of any assistance I could to the Chilean and Argentine governments; and to make reports on anything and everything I considered of interest. I retained enough caution to remind myself that it couldn't be as good as all that sounded. But it was, and the people, the country, the wildlife and the streams themselves were all so far beyond my expectations that I find myself with a story that needs to be told. It was a fisherman's winter without equal in my experience, a delight of travel and discovery that I know is worth sharing.

I left Seattle on a rainy Monday afternoon in early December, changed planes at Los Angeles and flew through the long night over Mexico, with only an occasional cluster of lights far below marking life in the darkness. Early next morning we landed in Guatemala

City, and already North America, as Canadians and
Americans know it, was far behind. We had flown in
past sharp volcanic cones, over lakes and jungle and
arid high land. Near the city one saw signs of increas-
ingly intensive agriculture in the high valleys and on
every plateau. From the air, which was all I saw of it,
Guatemala seems a fine city, well laid out and with some
handsome buildings, a big race track and plenty of playing fields. The airport was busy with peddlers and quick
little shoeshine boys, plump, brown, barefooted, flashing
smiles that won easy business. Vultures hovered over the
runways; steel-helmeted soldiers or police or both were
training or standing guard in troop carriers and small
tanks. Everything, even the soldiers, seemed informal
and remote, and it was hard to realize that one was
near a city that claims a population of nearly half a
million, perched in a hanging valley five thousand feet
above sea level.

From Guatemala it is a three-hour flight across Sal-
vador, Nicaragua and Costa Rica to Panama. It is a con-
fusing flight, southeastward, from Pacific to Atlantic to
Pacific again. From the air everything is beautiful—volcanic slopes, cultivated plains, fresh black lava flow, big
lakes, brilliant green swamps where the streams come
out to the sea. But it must be a hard and difficult country to live in and I was surprised at the intensity with
which it seemed to be used.

At Panama, one felt North American influence again,
and it was not unwelcome. With a delay of several
hours between planes, there was time to go up to the
new hotel, a magnificent building wide open to the
ocean winds. Above the ground floor it is nowhere

more than a single room in thickness, with an open,
tiled veranda on both sides of every room; the walls
and doors that open on these are built of wooden strips
that can be adjusted like the slats of a Venetian blind.
It was hot, with the heavy equatorial heat of Panama,
but there was every provision for coolness, including
a gleaming new swimming pool and a tree-shaded ter-
race, where soft-moving, graceful waiters brought any
drink in the world, mixed as it should be mixed. After
nearly twenty-four hours of flying one needed the rest
and was glad of it. But I was glad, too, when it was
time to go out to the airport again and board another
plane soon after midnight.

Flight is always exciting, a new way of seeing, yet
somehow unreal because it destroys time and distance
and, if all goes well, the physical hardships of travel.
Yet some things are seen only in flight—the enormous
sweep of the prairies, for instance, or the lake-dotted
reach of the barren lands in summer, great river deltas
like those of the Fraser and the Mackenzie, and the true
immensity of mountains. In the next day's dawn I could
see white clouds below, ranging forever out into the
west, broken only occasionally by the brown humps of
rock peaks, like barren islands seamed with waterless
watercourses. Eastward I saw a range of brown mountains just above cloud level, then another at wing level.
Beyond these was yet another, enormous, snow-covered,
set against the sun—the high Andes, piled out of the
Pacific to make the immense curved rim of the Amazon
Basin. It was a moment of breathlessness in which one
needed new words to replace all the superlatives of grandeur and magnificence one has squandered so freely on

the Rockies and the Coast Range. It was a new scale, physical geography and a world's legend suddenly made visible in snow and ice that would one day find its way through steaming jungle, two thousand miles and twenty thousand feet down to another ocean.

Lima should have been an anticlimax, yet was not. We swept in low over the rich, irrigated land, scattering chickens in the backyards of houses on the edge of the city. It is a white city, patterned and clean and handsome from the air, five hundred feet above the Pacific's white break on long beaches and brown cliffs— the city of the kings, the original heart of European civilization in South America, full of a grandeur that has survived and grown through earthquake and fire and invasion. Even Lima's airport does not betray her. It is broad and fine, with a magnificent terminal of marble, the most adult conception of an airport terminal I have seen anywhere. There were planes of various South American airlines coming and going at the same time as our own, and I watched the lively, affectionate, well-dressed Spanish people at their farewells and welcomings. It was clear, and more than clear to me, that I had come to another continent.

Lima is twelve degrees south of the equator. The border between Chile and Peru is a little over seventeen degrees south. I am not sure exactly when we crossed it, but it must have been rather over an hour after leaving Lima. The land below was sandy desert, with occasional strips and patches of cultivation where some source of water permitted irrigation. To westward the lazy Pacific rollers washed the beaches. In the east were the mountains, huge and dry and brown, with waterless streambeds and occasional distant snow peaks. As we went on even the little patches of cultivation disappeared and the land became the driest desert in the world, where rain has not fallen within living memory.

Chile is a long land, nearly three thousand miles long from north to south, and averaging only a little over a hundred miles wide, between the ocean and the peaks of the Andes. Here at the northern border I was still fifteen hundred miles from my trout-fishing country, yet below me, in the ocean a few miles offshore, is some of the finest big game fishing to be found anywhere—black marlin of over a thousand pounds, swordfish of over eight hundred, Allison's tuna of over two hundred and fifty, and some of them were to become world's records within the next few months. The black marlin record of that time was a fish of well over 800 pounds. Within four or five months it became 1025, 1060, 1090, 1135; and by August of 1953, the next year, it had almost doubled at 1560 pounds.

The bone-dry deserts and gigantic fish have a superficial connection in the Humboldt current. The current itself swings out of the Antarctic almost against the southern coast of Chile and strikes northward to Peru and eventually the equator. It is a hundred or a hundred and fifty miles wide, constantly fed by upswellings from the ocean depths and so unfailingly cold—no warmer than 55-60° F even in the tropics. It carries with it, as cold currents do, an enormous wealth of food and is the hunting ground of fish and bird life beyond count or calculation.

The coldness of the current creates cold cloud masses which ride the cold breezes toward the hot land. The

upward thrust of warm air from the land pushes them
higher and higher as they cross the sandy coastal plain
and holds their moisture suspended as they climb. So
they pass over the dry westward slopes of the Andes
to find the cold peaks and spill their moisture at the
headwaters of the Amazon.

From the air, the effect of all this is plainly visible.
For miles upon miles the coastal plain is bare and dry
—no stream reaches it from the high hills, even the
deepest gully of the hills themselves is dry. Then there
is a touch of green at the foot of the hills where some
great valley reaches the plain and its invisible stream
is turned to irrigation. As the valleys pass, irrigation
spreads farther and farther across the plain before each
stream is lost in the thirsty sand and the dry air. At
last a stream reaches all the way and spills a tiny waste
of water back into the ocean. Another succeeds and
still another, until the enormous valley of Aconcagua,
highest peak in the Western Hemisphere, opens up and
the plane lets down to the sudden spread of the City of
Santiago.

All things in Chile start from Santiago, "the Capital,"
Santiago de Chile, as Chileans proudly and properly call
it. Santiago is a city of one and a half millions, risen
astonishingly from the deserts, and from a total national
population of only five and a half millions. By American standards it is a very old city—over four hundred
years old in its oldest parts—yet in many aspects it is
a new and splendid city. It is a gay and friendly and
attractive city, it is where important things happen in
Chile, and generally it is the traveler's introduction to
Chile. It was my own introduction and the place where

all my fishing was planned. I remember it most happily, so I shall write of it a little, even though by doing so I delay the approach to those lovely southern rivers.

The Capital

I HAD DONE MY BEST TO LEARN WHAT I could of Chilean fishing from guidebooks and other more or less reliable sources before leaving Canada. I had the advice of my good friend George Andrews, who warned me on no account to miss the big fish of his favorite rivers—Enco and Laja, Tolten and San Pedro. Eddie de Rothschild, another trusted fishing companion, had written me to be sure to fish Maihue Lake and the Calcurrupe River.

I knew that trout had been first introduced to Chile in 1904 and that the principal species were European brown trout and rainbows. I knew of a report in the scientific literature that Pacific salmon had been successfully introduced, and I had been asked by a Canadian scientist to check on this. Some of the guidebooks mentioned steelhead or sea-running rainbows, and I knew attempts had been made to introduce Atlantic salmon, Sebago salmon and eastern brook trout. I could see from the map that Chile had a great many fine lakes and streams in the latitudes where one would expect to find trout, and I had heard many tales of very big fish. But I had not the slightest idea how to select from all this wealth of opportunity or how to find my way amongst it. I could speak no Spanish and I had a somewhat special problem—that of sampling the widest possible range of fishing waters in a rather limited time.

I need not have worried. Anglers everywhere are generous with information and advice, and I am inclined to think that the fishermen of Santiago are the most generous of all. It seemed, too, that everyone in Santiago was proud of "the South," of Chile's lake district, and that most of them manage to find their way down into it during the course of a summer. I learned first from Carlos Brunson and Doug Gorman of Panagra, then from Dennis Adamson of Esso, from Ray Grasty of Latour, and from Frederico Weisner of Sparta, the principal sporting goods store in Santiago.

Weisner, who has more than once captained the Chilean big-game fishing team, is a greater enthusiast for trout than for tuna and his store is a wonderful cleaninghouse for the most recent information from all over the south. The store, considering the problems of dollar exchange, carries a remarkable stock of every kind of gear, much of it of high quality and at prices that compare quite well with those of North American stores. Any fisherman who visits Chile will do well to pay a call on Frederico Weisner, whether he wants merely information and good fishing talk, or a complete outfit that will let him fish and camp in comfort anywhere in Chile, or just a few special local items. Frederico is an attractive and vivid man, lively almost to the point of excitability, and I sincerely regret that business kept him in Santiago while I was in the south, so that we never managed to fish together.

Frederico was determined that I must catch a really big Chilean trout as soon as possible and suggested, as did almost everyone else, that I start with Maule Lake and spoons, plugs or other hardware, because the fish there would take nothing else. This was a double disappointment to me, because I wanted to fish streams, not lakes, and had very little interest in trout, however large, that would not take a fly. But I was quickly reassured. Maule was the exception, a lake seven thousand feet up in the Andes, still in central Chile, and full of big rainbows. It is, in a sense, Chile's counterpart of Lake Titicaca, which lies at over twelve thousand feet on the borders of Peru and Bolivia, and where twenty-pound rainbows are common. I began to feel powerfully interested in Maule Lake, especially as M. S. McGoldrick, with whom I was to fish the Laja River, was planning to start for the Maule within a few days

Mac McGoldrick was one of a group of American and British fishermen in Chile who helped me in every possible way both in Santiago and in the south. I should like to name them all, as a gesture of gratitude, but second thought suggests that the gesture would be a greater satisfaction for me than for them; it might expose them, I'm afraid, to the importunate questioning of far too many North Americans who decide to chase trout in Chile. So they shall be nameless. But several of them met in a group one evening at the Carrera Hotel and skillfully planned my itinerary. Had it not been for their experience and knowledge of the ways of the country and its means of travel, I could not possibly have sampled as many waters as I did.

But I learned about more things than fishing and

travel in Santiago. It was there that I first began to get the feel of Chile and to realize the country's charm and difference. Chile calls herself the gringo of South America, and not without reason. Her people have an easy, outgoing friendliness, not altogether unlike that of North Americans, and a pioneer spirit that manifests itself not merely in ready hospitality but in a delighted surprise and pride in the country itself and the nation it has made them. They have also a natural courtesy, a sophistication and a concern for other nations that are not at all North American—and these qualities I found common to peasant and lord of the manor, to chambermaid, banker, boatman or carabinero. Chileans, to make an outrageous generalization, seemed to me essentially happy people who wanted others to be happy with them.

I remember now, with great happiness, the discoveries of the daytime drives with Dennis Adamson into the country around Santiago. One was swiftly free of the great city, and here was the vale of Chile, lovely irrigated farm lands, tiled cottages with gardens full of blazing geraniums, handsome houses with cool, flower-filled courtyards and delicate wrought-iron gates under arches, water-filled ditches flowing everywhere and great mats of blackberry vines, called the curse of Chile, making the hedgerows.

On the roads one met huge tank trucks, wooden instead of metal, carrying wine instead of gasoline. On the dusty side roads, and on dusty tracks beside the main roads, were horsemen, horse-drawn wagons and oxcarts. The farms everywhere were lovely, old and cherished and rich. As often as not the roads passed between great avenues of Lombardy poplars or eucalyptus, planted long ago; magnificent sweet chestnut trees shaded the farm buildings and weeping willows, yellow-barked and graceful, marked the irrigation ditches.

From time to time we stopped, to visit country-living friends on small farms, to find a drink in the cool stone-floored club of some little country town, or simply to step out on to the roadside. I heard for the first time the queltegue's scolding call and recognized the excitable spur-winged plover that uttered it. I saw bandurrias, great curved-beaked ibises, black and white with rusty brown heads, for the first time, and heard their sharp exciting note; though I did not know it then, both birds are everywhere along the rivers of southern Chile and the sound of them, wherever I heard it, would now take me instantly back to Tolten or Liucura, Calcurrupe or Petrohue.

We talked of Chile as we traveled and wherever we stopped, in farmhouse or club or bar, and I began to feel I knew a little of what made the country—patriotism above all, founded in the flag and the liberation; the land and its early nineteenth-century liberators, San Martín of Argentina and Bernardo O'Higgins, the Chilean-born son of an Irishman; after that the Spanish-Indian blood of the great majority of the population, volatile yet reasonable, independent yet not beyond discipline. The heart and history of Chile are in Santiago, Valparaiso and the luxuriant vale of Chile. Much of her wealth is in the copper and nitrate mines of the north. Much of her beauty is in the lakes and volcanos and timberlands of the south. And her spirit is somehow compounded of all these things.

There is in Chile, as in most South and Central American countries, a truly shocking gap between the wealthy few and the poor multitudes. In the northern mines and to some extent in industrial Santiago and Valparaiso, higher wages have begun to close the gap. In the agricultural areas, where farm laborers still work for as little as fifty cents a day, it remains enormous. Yet one felt that it is in the spirit of the country to change all this by sense and by law, by vote rather than by revolution. The country does not feel static, and there is no despair in the people. Education is compulsory and literacy is almost universal; six thousand new schools have been built since the war, and they are good schools, well-planned and with an up-to-date curriculum. Hydro-electric plants and irrigation dams have been built and others are under construction. Social services of all kinds are being constantly improved. New manufacturing industries, within the power and need of the country, are slowly developing. Trucks and Caterpillar tractors are moving in among the oxen of the southern logging operations. It is difficult to believe that the changes will not be sufficiently fast and thorough to be contained within that framework of democracy upon which Chileans pride themselves.

Perhaps all this seems beyond the scope of a fishing book. Yet I do not think I should enjoy fishing in a country whose hopes and aspirations were unknown to me or whose people seemed remote from me. I found Chileans everywhere welcoming and confiding and enthusiastic, and this was important to me, as it must be to anyone who goes there. By deliberate choice and planning, I spent one evening alone in Santiago, and that too became later a part of my fishing pleasure, even though I did little more than walk the streets and eat a first-class dinner.

Chile lives late and eats late. There is the long pause for siesta in the middle of the day, and after that stores and offices work through until seven or later. Any time before nine-thirty or ten o'clock is early for the evening meal.

I started from the hotel soon after nine one evening to walk—or rather wander—to a famous restaurant a mile or so away. It was a little before Christmas, close to the southern midsummer's day, and so still light. The streets were full and lively, full of traffic, full of walking people who seemed both happy and purposeful. One crosses Santiago streets with reasonable caution; traffic doesn't wait for pedestrians, even on the change of a light; it blows an assortment of horns and charges. On the big boulevard cars shifted from lane to lane without warning, driving fast or slow or in between, with lights or without them. A fine new car chose its moment and made a screaming U-turn at an intersection; approaching cars screeched their own tires momentarily and then went on as though it were nothing unusual. I saw no accidents, then or at any other time in Santiago, though I suppose they must happen.

One important shopping street I followed was closed to traffic and people strolled contentedly along it, looking in at the store windows, talking, laughing, admiring each other. Beyond the stores the street was quiet and almost deserted. I saw an old building ahead, partly demolished, the wall that butted on to the sidewalk still ten or twelve feet high. There was no warning sign,

no protective fencing, but there was a scattering of
rubble on the sidewalk and I saw a cloud of brick dust
rising above the wall. I crossed to the other side of the
street and as I passed two or three bricks flew over the
wall and clattered in pieces on to the sidewalk. I as-
sumed that Santiago lawyers have not fully developed
their business and the idea gave me a pleasant sense of
security and ease. Let the passer beware. Let him keep
his eyes open and mind where he puts his feet. It all
seemed far more reasonable than suing the city because
a woman's spike heel catches in a grating or a streetcar
starts with a jerk.

Yet there was plenty of law on the streets, smart
white-uniformed carabineros carrying white night sticks,
brown, disciplined, courteous men, proud of their force
and incorruptible. They interfered with no one, yet
they seemed very alert and where they controlled traffic the traffic obeyed with tight precision. No doubt
there is much petty legislation in Santiago not in evidence that evening, but it was obvious that its emphases
are very different from those of our own petty legislation. Since the City of Santiago seems to work quite
comfortably, even as do our own cities, it struck me
that all petty legislation is a burden on the people, an
offense against living.

I found my restaurant and dined well on Chilean
lobster and filete, with half a bottle of white wine and
half a bottle of red. An attentive waiter talked me out
of a three-colored ball-point pen, as I felt he had a
right to—with it he could be a hero for some brief
hour or two, whereas I could never be more than a
note-taking writer. A lovely brown-skinned girl sang

deep-voiced South American songs with a good orchestra. She was a part of the orchestra, and remained with them even when she was not singing, playing maracas or the pandareta. The effect was natural, effortless and authentic. Once while I was there she left the room and the whole orchestra left with her. Three minutes later she was back, smoothing a different dress that she seemed to have entered by some magic process. Her bare brown back, above the white material of the dress, was fleshed to the exact infinity that makes bones liquid and starts dimples. She swayed her hips to the music's start, smiled once and then her voice was filling the room again, its deep tones touching the table to vibration under my hand.

It was after 1:00 A.M. when I began to walk slowly back to the hotel. The streets were still full and lively and lighted. A group of us stopped to watch and advise as a girl struggled to kick life into a great shining Indian motorcycle. There were little temporary booths selling Christmas toys and favors all along the Boulevard O'Higgins. Near the O'Higgins statue someone was setting off fireworks, magnificent rockets that swished up and burst far above the rooftops. A carabinero came up as we watched and watched with us, laughing. Then he spoke a few words with the operators, still smiling and in great good humor, and there were no more fireworks. He may have told them to stop, but I think they were simply out of ammunition.

I sat awhile on a stone bench under O'Higgins' bronze horse, watching people and scrawling notes. No one bothered me or paid the slightest attention. The Boulevard O'Higgins is a noble street, so noble that I

began to wonder about its width, and I solemnly paced
it out. On either side is a good broad sidewalk and
three-lane roadway. The center strip is sixty-five yards
from curb to curb, with two avenues of trees and a
clear way between them about twenty-five yards wide.
It was in this space that the Christmas booths and cafés
and displays were set up.

I walked a little farther and came upon a commercial fisheries display—small boats and nets and other
gear, some salt-water fish and a few sad-looking but
attractive penguins.

Even at 2:00 A.M., when I turned off O'Higgins, the
shopping streets were bright and lively. I found my
way into a beautiful street of ancient buildings, clois-
ters and gardened courts. It seemed to be mainly doctors' offices, presumably with living quarters overhead,
and my footsteps echoed too loudly on the tiled side-
walks. I was within two or three blocks of the hotel
and the Plaza de la Constitucion, yet I heard roosters
crowing false dawn. The city was by no means asleep
—even in the street of the doctors' offices I heard footsteps other than my own. But I felt the evening had
been good to me. I had to fly to Buenos Aires the next
day to arrange an itinerary in the Argentine lake district, so I sought out my own bed while the roosters
still crowed.

The Lake of Big Rainbows

MOST FISHERMEN WHO GO TO CHILE try Maule Lake. It is a show place, about a day's drive from Santiago and a certain producer of big fish. "You must go there," Frederico Weisner told me, "so that you can be sure to see what a big Chilean rainbow looks like. But you must take spoons. They will not rise to flies."

Mac McGoldrick, Henry Gardiner and I left for the lake in the afternoon of December 28, which would be June 28 in the Northern Hemisphere. We were in Mac's panel truck with a Higgins trailer behind, and we had a good paved road to Talca, about two hundred miles south of the capital. From there we swung eastward along a graveled road that climbed slowly toward the Andes. The Maule River rushed in broken white rapids beside the road, heavy with snow water, and the road itself grew narrow and rough and twisting. We camped for the night beside a little stream at about two thousand feet—at the start, Mac said, of the really bad road.

When we went to sleep I had supposed we were in fairly remote and unpopulated country. The soil was volcanic and dry, growing scrubby bushes and a few small trees, and we had passed no settlements or houses for many miles. But as I went down to wash at the creek next morning I saw a stealthy movement in the brush and found I was watched by a ragged, dark-faced man under a black sombrero. He was not alone. Without serious search I found three or four other watching faces at a distance of fifty or a hundred feet from where I was crouched by the stream. They kept appearing and disappearing, nearer or farther away, all the while we were eating breakfast, just watching, without sign of friendliness or hostility. "They are waiting till we go," Mac said, "to see if we leave anything behind. There must be a farm somewhere near."

"What do they expect to find?" I asked.

"Anything or nothing. They're more curious than hopeful, but they'd probably steal quickly enough if they got the chance. You must never go off and leave a camp in Chile the way you do in Canada. Lock everything up in the truck or the trailer."

We left some food behind when we broke camp and no doubt it was found. The road, as Mac had warned us, became worse as it began to climb the last five thousand feet to the lake. In most places it was little more than a car's width, often with a precipitous drop on one side and with curves so steep that Mac had to ease the trailer around them. An irrigation dam was being built at the outlet of the lake, which should have meant heavy traffic, but we met little or nothing and were only slowed once or twice by trucks hauling equipment. By 9:00 A.M. we had reached the lake and chosen our campsite between two small creeks that entered near the outlet.

Maule Lake, Laguna del Maule, to give its proper local title, is reputedly at an elevation of eight thousand feet. My aneroid barometer made it a little over seven thousand feet, as did two other barometers Mac

was carrying in the truck. It is a considerable sheet of
water, at least six miles long, divided by a narrow neck
about a mile and a half from the outlet; it increases
steadily in width from this neck to the upper end,
where it spreads in two arms, but the average width
of the main lake is about two miles. It is set in alpine
desert, bare, dusty hills of pumice and volcanic sand,
with outcrops of laval rock and many great white
banks of snow. Wherever streams ran down from the
snowbanks there was green grass and flowers, and where
the watercourses spread at the lake's edge there were
rushes. It was exciting country to see and to be in; I
wanted to go out into it, to touch the snowbanks and
wade the creeks and fish the lake.

There were no boats on Maule at that time and the
road extended only a little way beyond the small weir
at the foot of the lake. Distances looked short in the
clear air and under the bright sun, and the open hills
seemed to offer good walking. Henry had been to the
lake once or twice before and he suggested that we
should walk to a creek mouth about four miles up along
the north shore of the lake. The first small section of
the lake, on which we were camped, was said to hold
only a few large fish, still dark from their spawning.

Henry, who was raised on the rangelands of Mon-
tana, was a good guide. He worked us up into the hills,
away from the edge of the lake, as quickly as possible,
and lined the low saddles between the hills to bring us
out as directly as possible to his chosen place. But it
was scorching hot under the bright sun and the sandy
ground made hard walking. We were glad enough to
come at last to a long, slow slope that led down to the

creek mouth, and we even found time to sit down and rest for a moment or two when we reached the lake.

Henry and I put up our rods while resting. Mac had decided not to fish; he is a convinced fly fisherman, and the idea of catching fish, however large, on hardware, did not appeal to him. Henry is a spinning enthusiast and had no such scruples; I had my orders to come to grips with a big Chilean rainbow and I did not feel I knew enough to justify me in slighting local advice to use hardware, so I had a light casting rod and a small Silex reel. I had not even ventured to bring a fly rod up the lake with me.

Henry started out with a brass and copper spoon and quickly hooked and lost a good fish. I put on a small plug, somewhat like a fly-rod flatfish and watched several good rainbows follow it in, pull at it and go free. So I changed to a small bronze spoon and almost immediately hooked and killed a bright twenty-seven-inch female that weighed nine and a half pounds. She fought quite well for a fish hooked on a spoon and seemed bright and in excellent shape, but I was shocked to find she still had a lot of loose eggs in her. I was even more surprised to find that her stomach was simply crammed with fresh-water "shrimp" (Gammarus limnaeus or something very close to it) with a scattering of snails, midge larvae, fresh-water clams and scarlet copepods—almost exactly the sort of feed one might expect to find in a really good Kamloops trout lake. I was immediately convinced that it must be possible to take fish on the fly, but there was little to be done about it then, as we were two long hours of walking from the truck.

I felt disappointed that my first Chilean trout should
have been a spawner, but it occurred to me that one
could expect little else of rainbow trout at seven thousand feet in a month corresponding to June. I wondered if we could hope to find any clean fish at all.
Henry settled that almost at once by hooking a lovely
maiden fish of five and a half pounds which fought
magnificently, jumping again and again through the
windy surface of the lake. I don't think I have ever
seen a finer rainbow, thick-flanked, firm and bright as
a fresh-run steelhead. Again, the stomach was full of
gammarus and other small feed; it was obvious that the
fish would come to a fly if one could reach them with
it.

We fished on slowly along the lake shore, hooking
and releasing a number of fish between four and seven
pounds, some bright and clean, some near spawning,
but all of them fat and in excellent condition. It was a
lovely day, with hot sun and a hot, dry wind, but the
little creeks we crossed below the snowbanks were ice
cold and the lake itself was only 51° F at the surface.
Once the steepness of the shore line forced us away
from the lake and up on to a high ridge. From it we
could see sunken islands and broad shallows and the
great brown weed banks that followed both shore lines
at a distance of a hundred and fifty feet or so from the
water's edge.

"Why don't we try the far side tomorrow?" I asked.

"It's supposed to be not much good," Henry said.
"Too deep."

"It looks to have a more gradual slope than this side,"

I objected. "And it can't be deep all the way. You can see the weed banks from here."

Henry's enthusiasm for exploration was at least as great as his love of fishing. Besides, you could see the dark masses of the weed beds dimly under the wind-broken surface of the lake. "I'd like to try it. I've never been over there."

"We'll make a day of it," Mac said. "And you can take fly gear—no hardware."

We had checked the temperature at 96° in the shade toward the middle of the afternoon, but there was four or five degrees of frost that night and I found a cotton-filled Chilean sleeping bag none too warm. We were up around six the next morning, cooked a quick break-fast and started on our journey.

The first obstacle was a wide, deep bayou of a creek mouth, not far from our camp, which led us hard back against the hills to a waterfall that forced out of the solid rock below a big snowbank. It was a lovely place, with a fine pool at the foot of the falls, but we saw no fish along the creek or in the pool, which I took as an encouraging sign that the main spawning run must be over. We crossed the snowbank above the falls, then a steep rock slide, and held elevation from there above a series of springs to a distant saddle, which led us over into a lovely green valley a thousand feet above the lake. A tightly enclosed torrent rattled between the green banks of the valley floor and made us search for a safe place to jump across it. Henry said that what we had seen already was worth the whole trip, and Mac and I agreed with him. The lonely little valley was in its alpine spring, a brilliant yet delicate contrast to the bare, dry hills all about us, where scattered black obsidian gleamed like huge diamonds in the sunlight.

We eased down gradually from the valley to where a second and larger creek entered the lake through a wide estuary. A flock of sheep or goats were grazing there, with two horsemen on the hills, watching them. "There are puma," Mac explained. "And human thieves as well, perhaps."

A few geese were feeding or standing out on the swampy ground near the creek mouth, the males conspicuously white-headed and white-breasted, with black beaks and black legs, the females barred and gray—they were Upland or Magellan geese, according to Peter Scott's key, and I saw them again many times, in both Chile and Argentina. Beyond them, at the edge of the lake, were good numbers of ducks which I could not satisfactorily identify, though I believe some of them were Chilean brown pintails and the larger birds may have been bronzewings in some stage of eclipse plumage. Slow, fat snipe rose from underfoot as we walked and flew a little way before settling. I searched carefully for the flamingos we had spotted through the glasses from across the lake the day before, but they were not there.

As soon as we were across the creek mouth Henry went out on a point and began to fish a spoon in the shallow water. He quickly hooked a lovely fish of five or six pounds which we safely returned after a good fight. We decided to go on farther, to two long points we had noticed from the far side the previous evening.

It was easy going, along gravel beaches and pumice cliffs that rose some twenty feet from the lake edge.

Little tyrant birds with rusty red backs whisked tamely ahead of us. A tiny cactus was breaking lovely red flowers wherever we walked and quick little lizards were sunning themselves on all the rocks. At one place we were able to look straight down from the cliffs on to a shallow rock-floored bay that was partially enclosed by a line of huge boulders running out across its mouth. On the shallows a dozen or more huge trout were lying, some of them almost black, others obviously colored, still others apparently bright. Mac pointed down at the two biggest fish, one black, one pale. "They're twenty-pounders anyway," he said. "Do you think you could catch them?"

I remembered the experiences of the previous day. "They must be spawners," I said. "Let's try it somewhere else first. We can always come back."

Henry threw out a spoon from the top of the cliff, but the fish paid little attention to it, so we went on. I put on my waders out at the end of the first long point, went into the water and began to throw a fly against the strong wind, working my way back along the sandy beach toward the pumice cliffs. It had seemed a good place when I started, but the wind was discouraging, limiting distance and drifting the fly back toward me faster than I wanted. I felt a fish pull at the fly, but it was a light take and I could not tell how large he was. Twenty or thirty yards farther on the same thing happened. I knew I would get results sooner or later, but I began to think of changing to some other place.

Henry was exploring his way ahead toward the second long point. Mac had wandered back to look again at the big fish under the pumice cliffs. I saw him coming toward me just as I rose and missed another fish.

"Come on down and try those big ones," he said. "I think you can do it. The wind will be half over your shoulder there and I'm sure it isn't too deep to wade."

So I went back with him. The fish were huge, all right, and some of them certainly looked clean enough. A few of the smaller ones moved occasionally, swam gently forward and out past the rocks into deep water. But most of them were very still and looked like anything but willing fish. They were all lying at much the same angle, facing more or less west, toward the upwind side of the bay. I climbed down and waded in. To my delight I could still see several fish, especially the darker ones, from the lower level. "If one of those black brutes comes up," I told Mac, "I'm going to pull it away from him."

Mac laughed. "Do what you like, but catch one, just to show it can be done."

I had been fishing a Carey's Special and I did not bother to change. The steady wind had set up a slow draw of current across the bay and the fly swung on it beautifully. The fish stirred at once as the fly passed near them, swam at it, even followed, but they would not take. I gave them three or four casts and the same thing happened each time. It was obvious I had to change, and being still convinced they were more interested in spawning than feeding, I decided on a bright orange fly I use a lot for steelhead, the Golden Girl. The effect was electric. From being mildly interested they suddenly became excited. Fish dashed about everywhere. Out of the excitement one struck hard at the

fly, right on the surface, and I pulled it away from
him. I missed fish again, on the next two casts, in exactly the same way—they were taking straight toward
me, in sudden rushes, and carrying the fly with them.
The next time I waited longer and set the hook firmly
as the fish turned. He fought for the rocks at once and
ran well out into the lake when I steered him past them.
He was a clean six-pounder, though not really bright,
and I weighed him in the net and returned him.

In the next two hours I hooked about a dozen big
fish and rose several others. Three or four threw the
fly. One, a big bright fish, took going away just as I
stripped in line to work the fly; that was an instanta-
neous break. Six others, all between six pounds and eight
and a half pounds, I landed and released. The eight-
pounder took in the deep water outside the rocks and
kept me busy for at least ten minutes. Like all the others,
he fought hard for the rocks when I brought him in
close, but I had learned by this time that I could wade
pretty well out there and use the length of my rod to
keep the line free.

Mac kept reminding me that the two biggest fish were
still there and that they were at least twenty-pounders
—the bright one he thought might be twenty-five. I
could see the dark fish clearly most of the time and I
knew he had started after the fly several times, but he
wouldn't give in to his excitement and grab it as the
other fish did. As a matter of fact I didn't particularly
want him to; so far I had avoided hooking any of the
really dark fish. But I told Mac, "From now on it's the
big ones or nothing."

I began to put the fly over them, throwing it well

outside and letting it swing in on the wind current. The black fish, which was the only one I could see, showed very little interest beyond a slight movement as the fly passed. I heard Mac call to me and looked up to see two splendid flamingos fly past on graceful wings, black-tipped and salmon-red in the sunlight. I watched until they pitched over on the far side of the lake, then I put the fly over the big fish again. This time I began to work it with a fast strip as it came near them. The black fish started up and began to follow. I kept stripping. There was a tremendous swirl, then my line was running out as though it were hooked to a runaway train.

I didn't really want the fish, so I let him take it, right out between the two biggest rocks, and I didn't bother to move down fast, as I had with the other fish, to keep it clear. He swung over, wedged the line under the rock and broke me before I could clear it. I looked up at Mac and grinned. But he wasn't grinning. "What did you let him do that for?" he asked.

"He was awful black. I didn't want him," I said.

Mac is a very kindly and temperate man. "It wasn't the black fish. It was the bright fish. A twenty-five-pounder on the fly. You would have been the hero of Chile."

Now I *saw* the black fish take. I watched him all the way, even felt a little ashamed at the last moment for letting him take. But Mac was up on the cliffs, looking right down on the whole business, and he still sticks to his story. The bright fish cut in at the last moment and had it. I'm afraid I believe him.

But I was happy enough as I took off my waders and all through the long walk back to camp. It was a lovely evening as the wind died away, and we made a good supper with a good red wine. A young moon hung briefly over the mountains as we talked afterward; then there was only the Southern Cross and the Galaxies above it.

The Laja River—Anglers on Horseback

I UNDERSTAND THERE ARE BOATS ON
Maule Lake now, and that the road has been extended
for some distance up along the south side. I suppose
progress is being made on the dam, though I have not
heard that the lake has been raised yet. It seems fairly
certain that the dam will have an adverse effect on the

fishing. The spawning area in the creeks will certainly
be reduced. The present shallows and extensive weed
beds will be buried under a considerable depth of water
and will become much less productive. The shallows
created at the lake's new level may be equal in area to
those that are lost, but since the lake will be drawn
down each summer they are not likely to become highly
productive. The lake is already a great plankton producer, and I doubt if it will be greatly improved in
this respect. But dam or no dam, there will always be
some fish there and they will be big fish.

If I were to fish the lake again in its present state,
I should choose February or March, because nearly all
the big fish would be well recovered from their spawning by then. And I should hope to have a boat. I feel
quite certain that there must be times when a big fly
worked along the edges of the great weed beds would
take fish extremely well. It would be difficult to say
too much for the present quality of the fish in the
lake. The great majority seem to spawn for the first
time as three-year-olds. A maiden two-year-old weighed
five and a half pounds, a three-year-old that had spawned
once was six and a quarter pounds and a four-year-old
that had spawned twice was nine and a half pounds.
No doubt many individuals grow even more rapidly
than this suggests.

But Maule Lake, good as it is, is by no means the
best of Chilean fishing, nor is it in any way typical.
The wonder of Chile is that her rivers, not her lakes,
are the great trout producers. Much as I had enjoyed
the lake and the strange alpine, volcanic country around
it, I was not altogether sorry when the time came to

move on southward again toward the Laja River, which I was to fish next with Mac McGoldrick.

Unfortunately Henry had to leave us at Talca to go back to Santiago and attend to the affairs of the Anaconda Copper Company. Mac and I drove on toward Chillan for four and a half hours over the bumpy, dusty, wandering main roads of central Chile, reaching the very comfortable Gran Plaza Hotel at about ten-thirty on the night of December 31, 1951. Chillan is a city of only fifty or sixty thousand people, and it was largely destroyed by an earthquake in 1939, but we had a far better cooked and better served dinner that night than I am ever able to find when traveling through a North American city of comparable size. I learned later to expect good food in the provincial cities of Chile, but after the simplicities of Maule even Mac, who is fairly spartan about his creature comforts, was moved to say, with a smile, "That was a good dinner, wasn't it?" A few minutes later, as we were going up in the elevator, the New Year came in with a burst of whistles and fireworks and cheering in the handsome square outside the hotel.

The next morning we drove south for another three or four hours to the Palacio, a comfortable lodge on the bank of the Laja, cherished and maintained by Mac and T. N. Chambers and a few other enthusiasts who love the big river. For much of the way we followed "The Great All-American Highway," proudly announced by printed signs. Its surface varied from finely powdered red dust, axle-deep in places, to occasional patches of freshly spread gravel about the size of cobblestones. Some of the bridges were precarious wooden structures,

held together by a haphazard patchwork of shaggy
cables and steel plates and bolts, all obviously added
from time to time as the immediate prospects of collapse seemed to suggest. A few looked so doubtful to
Mac that he preferred to take the truck down the
wagon trails and through the fords. Other bridges
were new and handsome concrete structures, but these
were usually incomplete or with unfinished approaches,
so that we had to turn again to fords or temporary
structures of planks and cribbing.

It was a fine day and very hot, well up in the nine-
ties. The powdery dust filtered into every nook and
cranny of the truck. The heavy duty springs put solid
impact into every jolt. Yet it was an exciting and satisfying drive. We met practically no other motor vehi-
cles, but many oxcarts hauling hay or wood, and in-
numerable horsemen on neat, well-groomed little horses.
They were proud-looking men for the most part, handsomely dressed and firmly settled in their great sheepskin saddles. Nearly all of them wore broad sombreros,
dress silk ponchos of many colors and matching sashes.
Most of them had the traditional carved wooden stirrups and spurs with two- or three-inch rowels.

Sometimes we had to pass herds of sheep and cattle
and the riders always drove hard to clear the road.
Once I saw a horse slip and stumble so far that its
rider's foot must have touched the ground, but it recovered in some miraculous way, almost without losing
its stride, the man stayed in the saddle and a moment
later they were herding the animals as though nothing
had happened. Both Mac and Henry, who are horsemen
themselves, had some reservations about the Chileans as

horsemen. But I was impressed by the neat, handy appearance of the light-boned horses and their invariable good temper, as well as by the graceful, easy way that everyone, man, woman and child, seemed to have in the saddle. Again and again in Chile I saw five- or six-year-old urchins perched up in the broad sheepskin saddles of big horses, kicking them along at a gallop, often with a still younger brother or sister hanging on behind.

The villages we passed were quiet and peaceful but obviously poor, with few stores and those few extremely simple. The country was nearly all agricultural and for the most part irrigated, a rolling but not hilly land that stretches for sixty or eighty miles between the Pacific Ocean and the foothills of the Andes. It had been settled for a long while. Often the road was bordered by magnificent avenues of eucalyptus and poplars, a hundred or a hundred and fifty feet tall, and chestnuts and other imported shade trees were just as magnificent.

We left the main road at Yungay and passed through the little villages of Huepil and Tucapel. Mac stopped to buy bread in Tucapel, but we could find no meat in either place. It was then Mac told me that the agricultural laborer of central Chile is paid about fifty cents a day, a wage that will support him only if he grows some sort of subsistence on his own patch of land. There is little demand for the butcher shops to supply, little energy in the food the people eat, little production in the work they do—and so, little return to buy the nourishment that would make for better production. To an outsider, this seems tragic, wasteful and by no means impossible to change. Yet an outsider will not easily find discontent or unhappiness in Chile; he will find optimism, pride, humor and a very real joy in living, especially among the poorer people. I thought of this often as I moved about the roads and railroads and rivers of Chile, and I wondered if the quality of civilized happiness one finds there now can maintain itself through the changes that are sure to come.

Mac was disappointed when we reached the Palacio to find that the river was far above normal height. How high it was even he did not fully realize until the next day, when we rode several miles upstream to start fishing at the Palisades Pools. The river was huge there, tearing down in tumbled green and white water that seemed to offer no place at all for a fish to hold. I fished the edges of the broken water, but could find nothing.

Mac and I fished for five days on the Laja. The high water made us work much harder for the fish we caught, and I haven't the least doubt it kept us from catching more fish and considerably bigger fish. But I have a thousand vivid memories of the river, all of them happy, and after each day there I felt washed clean by wholly new experiences.

Perhaps the best days were those when we rode upstream from the Palacio. We would leave at seven-thirty or eight o'clock, Mac on his big red horse, Tucapel, myself on a neat, patient bay mare, Estrella; our two secretarios, as Mac called them, on their own horses behind us. The secretarios were sixteen-year-old boys, Arturo and Santiago, shy, delightful children, ready to laugh at the least provocation, quick and intelligent and sympathetic. They knew the river valley—every pool and ford and branch—intimately, though no better, I

think, than Mac knows it. They could give local names
for nearly all the birds and trees and plants we saw and
Arturo, who was Mac's regular secretario, knew more
than a little about the fish. I was Santiago's first assignment.

The floor of the Laja Valley above the Palacio is a
great boulder-strewn flat, cut by many channels and
half a mile or more in width. We did not follow the
river, but held to high ground on the right bank, along
roads and trails two or three hundred feet above the
valley floor. We passed a few small farms, perched somewhere on the slope, and Mac usually stopped at one or
another to pay a courtesy call or buy vegetables for
dinner, and usually came back with some complimen-
tary apples for lunch.

Somewhere beyond the last farm the Palisades—three-
or four-hundred-foot cliffs—close in on the valley and
we turned down the steep slope. So we came to the
first ford, a little arm of the river not much over knee-
deep for the horses, but with a bottom of smooth round
boulders that seemed to me to mean trouble. Mac crossed
on Tucapel without so much as a backward glance. I
watched the big horse do the thing so easily, placing
his feet carefully, without haste, yet by no means slowly.
Then I eased the little mare in and she did it just as
well for me, so I decided to say nothing. The next ford
was far more formidable—still only a branch of the main
river, but a sizable river in itself and with a really sav-
age run of current. Tucapel went in again, a little more
slowly this time, but just as calmly and confidently.
The water built on Tucapel's flanks, then up to the
saddle flaps, so that there was a hump in the river above

him and a sharp drop below. The mare followed him
calmly and I felt her solid under me all the way even
though she was edged downstream a little when we
came to the fullest force of the current.

I kicked her up alongside Tucapel when we were
across and asked Mac, "What about all these boulders?
I should think the horses would slip and break their
knees."

Mac laughed. "They were raised right here in the
valley," he said. "They've spent their whole lives running over the rocks and fording the branches to find
food. They'll take care of you. I wouldn't be afraid
to swim the main river with Tucapel. I think Arturo's
done it. They're water horses."

After that I took as strong a delight in what the
horses could do as in the fishing. Without them we
should have had little or no fishing in that part of the
river, with the water at the height it was; we crossed
each day three or four major branches, some deep
enough to force even Mac's big horse into half-swim-
ming, half-walking for fifteen or twenty yards downstream. We forded again, many times, as we moved
from pool to pool. We climbed steep banks of rolling
gravel and went down others just as steep. Occasionally I waded too far and got into an uncomfortable
place; all I had to do was signal Santiago, who would
bring the horses down and help me out.

It was altogether fascinating to me to feel and watch
the little mare wading under me. She would test her
footing, even as I do when I am wading, and set each
foot down solidly and securely before shifting her
weight again. She leaned against the strong current,

even as I do, and occasionally stumbled and recovered, even as I do. Sometimes the current was too much for her and she turned down from it or was swept down for a little way, but she never lost her footing altogether and always climbed out in the end, completely calm and confident. She had four feet to my two, of course, proportionately more slender legs against the current, and a lot greater strength than mine. But she had no felt wading shoes and she was carrying a hundred and sixty pounds of me with assorted fishing gear and wet waders.

We did not go so far as to gallop the horses over the rocks of the river bottom, as I saw some young farm hands doing by the Laja one day. Nor did we actually fish from the horses, though I told Mac I thought we did a little ground-baiting with them; whenever our cavalcade crossed a ford we kicked the rocks around considerably and I haven't the least doubt that our passage stirred out a few crayfish that must have tempted a trout or two into feeding. One leading farmer of the valley, Don Pancho, with whom Mac fishes occasionally, actually does fish from his horse. He uses the native professional's gear—a twenty-foot bamboo pole, with twenty feet of strong line tied to the tip, a big hook and a big crayfish on the hook. The crayfish goes out like a fly, on an overhead cast, and is fished almost like a slack-line fly. When a fish takes hold, Don Pancho swings the horse around, sets the rod over his shoulder, claps in his spurs and rides off till the fish comes bumping on to the beach. He enjoys it enormously, and so does everyone who fishes with him.

All the days we fished on the Laja were beautiful,

with a high hot sun and a strong breeze. The snow-
covered cone of the Volcan Antuco and the still love-
lier twin peaks of Sierra Velluda, with the tumbled
cascade of broken blue ice between them, were visible
from most parts of the valley. Birds were everywhere.
We started bronzewing ducks and Chilean teal from
the backwaters. Once we almost rode on to a group of
bandurrias strutting and talking their goose notes. Mock-
ingbirds called from the bush and caught flies in the air.
Garza mayor, the white egret, swung on slow wings,
gleaming against the gray palisades. The white-tailed
kite, Bailarin, hovered and danced in the shimmering
heat. Pigeons and doves called from the high trees and
occasionally swept across the valley.

All these things were new and wonderful to me. And
so was the fishing. We were searching mainly for big
brown trout, which we knew would be feeding almost
exclusively on the crayfish, apancora, that is abundant
in nearly all Chilean streams. In the swollen, many-
branched river even Mac and Arturo did not know just
where to look for them, but we found enough to keep
us interested. On our best day we had seven fish between us averaging well over three and a half pounds,
and we released many that were just under the seven-
teen-inch, one-kilo limit that Mac likes to keep to on
the Laja.

I did not find it easy fishing. There was the strong
wind and the big river, of course, but that was not all;
I had a lot to learn. I started out by fishing an almost
dead fly, as I would for winter steelhead, imagining
that the fish took the apancora as they were swept
helplessly down by the current. Mac had to suggest

working the fly, which I did with a steady beat of the rod top and found almost immediately productive. But hooking the fish when they took was still a problem and it remained a problem that I was unable to solve properly through my whole stay in Chile.

A fish taking hard in the full swing of the fly was no problem, of course, but few of them did that. The browns especially seem to take apancora very cautiously, as though they are afraid of a nip from its claws. They follow, making gentle plucks, and to strike then means a fish hooked lightly in the point of the jaw or, more often, not hooked at all. I tried releasing a few coils of line from my hand, but that old trick, so often successful with Atlantic salmon and steelhead, was completely useless. One has to keep the fly moving in spite of the plucks, keep it moving until somehow the line shows an unnatural draw against the current. Then is the time to strike, and if the fish is not too directly below he should be well hooked.

I did not learn all this on the Laja, and for every good fish I killed there I lost two or three—often after a minute or two of holding them. It was annoying, but completely fascinating, and even now, two years later, I can recall every detail of a score of good fish that I almost hooked or hooked and lost in those days on the big river.

Generally we had to work hard for every fish we found during the heat of the day. But when the sun went down and the wind died, around 8:00 P.M., the good hour was on. It was the time to repair all the sins and errors of the day.

I remember the Fence Pool in the late evening light,

a rush of white water at the head and slackened flow
beyond it. Mac, with Arturo, was somewhere below
me. Santiago was with me, still a little shy because it
was the first day. I made a few casts at the broken
water to let out line, then reached over and put the
fly into the slack on the far side. Almost as it landed
a huge brown trout came right out in the evening light
and crashed back, head first, with the fly in his mouth.
I tightened gently and for perhaps fifteen seconds I had
him. Then he was gone. He would not come again, but
three or four casts downstream a three-pounder took
firmly and held on.

The Laja River browns were good strong fish, in excellent condition. Big fish jumped right out at the fly
rather commonly, especially in the very fast water. This
was exciting, and so was the swirling take where the
bronze and gold of the fish showed in a sudden flurry.
Even a deep take nearly always boiled on the surface
and sent the heartbeat higher. Most of the fish jumped
at least once after they were hooked, a few jumped
several times, and all made good runs and put up a
heavy, dogged resistance. There are plenty of three- and
four-pound fish in the river and by releasing anything
under seventeen inches one can expect the catch to
average out at around three and a half pounds. Mac's
best fish on this trip was a shade under five pounds—
he called it four and seven-eighths. My own best was
just over four and three-quarters. All our four-pounders were maturing three-and-a-half-year-olds, which had
not previously spawned. Fish in the two- to three-pound
range were two-and-a-half-year-olds. It seems that a typical fish of the stream spawns for the first time at the

end of the fourth year, at a weight of about five pounds. The record fish caught from the Palacio is eleven and a half pounds, taken by Dr. Chambers in February 1948. Mac killed a fish of ten and a half pounds in March 1949 and at least two eight-pounders have been recorded. Undoubtedly there are always fish of this size somewhere in the stream; I judged the fish that jumped out with my fly to be at least seven, possibly eight pounds, and Don Pancho says there is an enormous fish, El Grande, somewhere just below the highway bridge. "But the river is too damn deep. You can't get at him." I liked that story because it is positive and complete and leaves no loophole for testing. But Mac wouldn't go along with it. "I doubt if El Grande exists," he said. "Or ever did exist."

Mac told me that rainbows were once common in the Laja, but that the run of the river is now about 95 per cent brown trout. This was true of our catch —Mac had one lovely rainbow of four pounds and I had one of two and a half, both of which made magnificent fights. But I occasionally stopped to fish what I called "nursery stretches," comparatively shallow runs where small fish were obviously on the feed. It was easy enough to take and release half a dozen fish of between twelve and seventeen inches in any of these places and I told Mac that the fish in this size range were at least 50 per cent rainbows. Since the brown is a fall spawner and the rainbow a spring spawner, it occurred to me that bad conditions at either season could very easily change the ratio from year to year. A year later Mac wrote me: "Your prognostication of the return of the rainbow has come true," and sent his fishing diary for the season which showed that the fish he kept, including one splendid seven-and-three-quarter-pounder, were running about 50 per cent rainbows.

But when I fish the Laja again, I do not think I shall care much whether the fish are rainbows or browns—in fact, I half-hope they are browns, if only because of the way they take and because they seem, if scale readings can be trusted, to be almost perfectly adapted to the stream. It was a brown trout, after all, that I took from the smooth, deep run under the cut-bank just as the good hour started on our last evening. And it was a brown trout that took, minutes later, in a fearsome swirl of churned-up water down near the tail of the pool. He jumped almost straight at me, then took off in a run that went down into the backing. After that things were quieter until Santiago, like an eager pup, started dancing on the beach and trying to grab for the line. I talked him out of it somehow, in spite of language difficulty, even as I had a dozen times before in our brief association. But when the big fish came in on his side it was too much for him. He grabbed the leader and heaved. The fish bounced up on the beach. The leader broke. The fish bounced back for the river again. Santiago plunged and grabbed, flipped the fish over his shoulder and all was well. We knelt opposite each other, laughing. I showed him how to put a finger in the gills of the fish. "Pescado, sí," I said several times. "Línea, no." He seemed to understand, and I hope he did, because I wouldn't like some later visitor to think I had taught him his own method.

We met Mac and Arturo a few minutes later and started the hour's ride home. The moon was bright, the

sun only a red remembrance in the west. We crossed
the fords in silver water, climbed the bank and splashed
along the narrow way that serves as both road and irrigation ditch. The poplars on either side of it were
enormously high above us, and silver black in the moonlight; water splashed and gleamed under the horses' feet;
dogs barked at the farm nearby. Estrella began to step
lively for home. We crossed the open meadows by the
lone poplar, passed through the pine forest with Mac's
white coat a faint blur in front of me and came out
to the road by a little lighted cottage. It was after ten
when we dismounted at the Palacio, time for a bath
and a drink of Scotch, then dinner with a good red
wine and Mac's companionship.

Some Incidental Things

ONE DAY WHILE WE WERE AT THE
Palacio, Mac and I drove fifty miles up the valley to
see Laja Lake. Mac knew the lake had been stocked a
few years previously and that some good fish had been
caught there, but the information was quite vague and
we made the trip as an exploration rather than as a fishing expedition.

The road along the valley was a good deal better
than most roads of central Chile, quite well graveled
and not too rough. It was built and maintained, we
learned, by the electrical company, Endesa, which owns
the Laja power plant. Occasionally we could see the

river, but always at some distance across a rough and rocky flat. Mac had hoped to find an easy way down to it from the road, but we found nothing on this day and Mac wrote me a year later that he had found the nearest road down to this upper part of the river on the opposite bank, above Trupan. It was a rewarding discovery, too, as he killed fourteen fish that day, nine rainbows and five browns, running from two and a half to a little over three pounds.

We passed through the quiet little village of Antuco, where there is a road down to a ferry across the river, and soon after came in sight of the power plant, Planta Hidroelectrica el Abanico, a fine modern-looking affair with six gleaming penstocks leading down to it over the long slope of the hill. I judged the head at four to six hundred feet and thought the penstocks about four or five feet in diameter. Clearly it did not begin to handle the river's potential, but just as clearly it was a big and important thing, probably well able to care for the fairly simple present needs of the big valley below it.

The road began to climb immediately we were past the plant and I saw that a canal circled the shoulder of a big bald hill to deliver the water to the penstocks— the hill was bald, Mac explained, because slides from it had damaged the canal, so the company had simply cleared away all the surface soil and gravel to bedrock. It seemed to me an impressively complete and practical solution.

We passed the dam, which was quite small and confirmed my impression that no effort had been made to store the Laja's enormous winter floods—or even the spring runoff that was still holding the river so high.

Just beyond it we met some friends on the way down. They told us they had camped at the lake for two or three days and explored it as thoroughly as they could without a boat, but had found no fish at all. They suspected this might be because the comparatively small numbers of fish that had been planted were all released over on the far side of the lake and had not yet had time to spread.

Mac and I decided to go on and see for ourselves, even though the news confirmed what we had expected. It was a gray day in the hills, with a cold wind blowing and clouds close above the twelve-thousand-foot peaks of Sierra Velluda. Mac drove the twisting road and I watched the static turmoil of blue green ice on the face of Velluda, wondering about it. I supposed it would be ten thousand years old, yet to be so old it must have survived tremendous volcanic heats from Velluda herself and nearby Antuco. From a distance the ice seemed delicate and lovely, light as the ruffles of a woman's blouse, yet it was not hard to imagine the ferocity of slopes and precipices, overhangs, crevasses and caverns one would find if one climbed there.

As we passed Velluda, Antuco came in sight, the first perfect volcanic cone I had seen at close quarters. There was a fascination in watching the smooth, symmetrical slopes, a restfulness for the mind that made me think of the gray walls of contemplation; it seemed a mood that could go on and on, growing steadily in depth and satisfaction and I understood for a moment the reverence that Tibetan monks feel for the high peaks that surround their monasteries. Then the road swung away from the base of the cone to find passage among the awesome black masses of the lava flow that had come from it only ninety years earlier. The lava extended clear to the lake shore, and entered the lake. When Mac stopped the car we looked back over an empty waste of gigantic furrows that seemed to have been plowed by a crazy plowman with a hundred-foot plow and a runaway team of hill-high horses.

The wind through the passes was cold and very strong. Whitecaps broke all over the surface of the lake and snow squalls swept across the mountains at its head. Laguna Laja is big for a mountain lake, perhaps twenty miles long with many big arms that cut back into the hills. It is at an elevation of a little under four thousand feet, and its whole shore line slopes a good deal more steeply than does the shore of Maule Lake. The January surface temperature was about 58° F —six degrees higher than Maule. We fished as best we could from the shore, throwing out against the hard wind, and I searched all through a narrow protected arm that averaged no more than ten or twelve feet in depth, but we did not see a fish of any kind. The lake bottom where we were fishing was coarse volcanic sand or else volcanic rocks, rough and broken, little worn by the water. Searching among these rocks along the water's edge I found a few gammarus and perhaps the greatest abundance of crayfish I saw anywhere in Chile. Every rock one turned seemed to harbor half a dozen or more, most of them of good size. The run of the lake shore on the far side and up at the head suggested good spawning streams, steadily maintained by snow and glacier water through the summer months. Laja may never be as great a trout lake as Maule or Titicaca, but it is difficult not to believe it will produce some wonderful fishing when the trout spread through it and start to work on the accumulated surplus of feed.

As we turned away from the lake toward the road we saw two smartly mounted carabineros riding along it. They saluted but kept moving, side by side and straight in the saddle as though on parade.

"What are they doing up here?" I asked Mac.

Mac pointed to the hills at the head of the lake. "There's a pass through there to Argentina," he said. "They'll be on the watch for smugglers—cattle mostly."

I saw these two-man mounted patrols again and again on the roads of Chile, especially along the lonely roads in the high mountains. They never passed without some courteous sign of recognition—for that matter, I cannot remember meeting anyone on the roads of Chile who did not pass the time of day—and if one stopped them they were always ready to smile and joke and ask with interest about the fishing. As we climbed into Mac's 1951 GMC truck I was beginning to realize that the pace and habits of rural Chile have many qualities that began to pass away from us in North America at least fifty years ago.

The day we spent at the lake was by far the easiest and quietest of the week I spent with Mac. At Maule we walked hard and fished hard in the hot sun and the dry wind. On the Laja we rode for two or three hours each day to get to our fishing and for another hour or so at the end of the day to get home. There was heavy wading to be done, much casting—and again, the brilliant sun and the hard wind. I am dark-skinned and have never before been much bothered by the sun, but the first day at Maule started the skin peeling from my face and by the time I left the Laja I had lost three or four skins, not only from my face, but from my hands and forearms as well.

In the afternoons on the river it was really hot; we checked the thermometer at 104° F in the shade one afternoon, and it fell to 48° F the same night. Immediately the sun went down one needed warmer clothes, and I found that to be the same everywhere in Chile; the solution is simply to carry a heavy sweater or coat and put it on as soon as the valley comes in shadow.

Another minor hazard of the Laja, and most Chilean streams in January, are the Coli-huachos. Chile has no mosquitoes, no blackflies, no really evil biting insects of any kind; I had heard this before I went there, I checked carefully under all sorts of conditions and I can affirm that it is so. The explanation, I suppose, is that the northern deserts are too dry and the fence of the Andes is too high and too cold for such creatures to pass. But there *is* the Coli-huacho, an over-sized horse-fly, black-bodied with a fierce orange face and stern; a slow, blundering, clumsy but persistent and abundant creature whose nuisance value is more serious than his bite. On the Laja, the Coli-huachos were allied with the Tabanos, small, rather pale deerflies. The Coli-huachos buzzed and bumbled everlastingly before one's face, always in the way as a fish rose or a difficult cast had to be made. They would bite if they had time, an annoying, fiery pinprick of a bite with little or no aftereffect, slyly delivered through the shirt and just behind the elbow. The Tabanos preferred to sneak in under one's hat or behind the ears; they were quicker, more skillful and far less distracting. Apart from these two, the only other biting fly I found in Chile was the Polco, a very small fly, not much larger than a no-see-um, which appeared on one or two rivers just at dusk and attacked with moderate persistence, though slowly and awkwardly. The Polco carries enough poison to raise a lump, but I never found him more than a mild nuisance.

When I think of the heat and the wind, the length of the days we put in and the Coli-huachos, I suppose I must have been uncomfortable at times on the Laja. But I cannot remember now that I was; it seems to me to have been a perfect time on a wonderful fishing stream and I was truly sorry when the time came to drive back to Chillan with Mac and get aboard the train for Temuco. I had the whole south before me and a dozen rivers of superlative reputation, but if Mac had been free and had said the word I would cheerfully have delayed with him in central Chile to fish not only the Laja, but the Nuble, the Diguillin, the Cholhuan and the upper reaches of the Bío Bío. Central Chile is not organized for the tourist fisherman as the south is, its scenery is less impressive, its climate tougher and its roads are less dependable, but it has some fine rivers and a lot of wonderful trout fishing.

The train from Chillan to Temuco was my first experience of Chilean railroads, but trains are the cheapest, most dependable and generally the most convenient form of transportation. One uses them a great deal.

My journey to Temuco was a matter of about five hours and some two hundred miles, through the full heat of the afternoon. By some skillful negotiation, Mac had reserved a seat for me. He also showed me how to get my baggage into the baggage car, how to tip the porters no more than five pesos a bag, and how to give the mustached, efficient-looking baggage man a hundred pesos to see that the baggage arrived at the other end —all points of wise travel that one can learn far more expensively, I am told.

After seeing the thoroughness of Mac's preparations in my behalf, I was a little apprehensive as to how I would make out on my own until I met my next traveling companion, Jacko Edwards, in Temuco. But I found my seat quite safely—No. 23 in a crowded day coach —and settled into the ancient black leather alongside a large Spanish lady who paid no attention to me at all. It was a pretty hot seat beside a wide open window through which the sun streamed in full glory. The train started smoothly and picked up speed very fast. I began to feel I was doing pretty well. Then my seat companion said something to me I did not understand. I did my best with it. That is, I smiled and nodded and looked very intelligent, but evidently I had the wrong combination because she repeated the words again, rather fiercely I thought. I hastily admitted that I did not speak Spanish. She turned abruptly away and gazed out of the window.

It was a temporary respite. A few miles further on she got hold of the conductor and told him something. He at once turned upon me and asked for my ticket. I showed it to him and he began to explain something, at first patiently, then despairingly. For once, there was no one nearby who spoke English. But I finally realized he was trying to tell me I was in the wrong seat—an

absurd notion, I thought, after the ease with which I
had found this one, obvious, right seat. I summoned my
fragments of Spanish and argued; I wasn't going to be
victimized by a large lady who didn't like to sit by me.
Several people in nearby seats joined in, in a helpful,
friendly way. And in the end I got the point. My seat
was No. 3 in aisle 2, not No. 23 at all. The conductor
led me to it, first chasing out an occupant, and settled
me there with soothing words. But I was remembering
my first ride in an American streetcar, when I stuffed
a transfer into the coin machine. That conductor approached things a little differently. "Okay, wise guy,"
he said. "Now just you take it out of there." And I
did, in the course of several blocks and not without difficulty.

Apart from this enforced recollection of a few difficult moments, my journey went smoothly and well. The
train ran at a great rate, but stopped quite frequently,
and every stop was a minor celebration. Whether or
not we had passengers to deliver, half the population
came down to meet us at every station, and it was, I
suspect, always the more colorful half. There were
peddlers and hawkers of all kinds, offering fresh fruit,
magazines, candy, rugs, sashes or rawhide work. There
would be a carabinero or two, a number of railroad
officials, shoeshine boys, many child porters in num-
bered red caps. All these had some obvious business to
be done or attempted, but they were in the minority.
Most of the people on the platforms had no obvious
business. Some may have been waiting for local trains,
a few were welcoming travelers, but for most the coming of the Expresso seemed a pleasant social occasion,

something to watch, a reason to mingle and meet with friends and acquaintances. And they were themselves something to watch. Country people for the most part, farm laborers, cowboys, farmers, millers and small merchants, nearly all of them wore some modification of horseman's dress and a good proportion were in the full glory of the Chilean huaso or cowboy.

A huaso at his best is probably the most handsomely dressed man in the world today. Everything he wears is functional, yet everything is decorative. Dark, tightly fitting striped pants look fine on a horseman and the same material looks well in London, at the diplomatic councils of the world, or striding the platforms of San Rosendo and Lautaro. A short black coat with skillful arrangements of buttons on back and sleeves, and a broad black sombrero go naturally with the striped pants, and the more timid variations one sees at Ascot or presidential inaugurations or fashionable weddings are not half so impressive. But the well-dressed huaso goes on from there to neat high-heeled boots, a striped silk sash of several colors that drip to swaying fringes at his left side, and a matching silk poncho, neatly folded and thrown over one shoulder. A few men like this, with others perhaps in brown or gray coats and pants and sombreros to match, make any crowd exciting to watch. But there were old men, too, some in full blanket ponchos and quiet, simple men in white shirts and old tweed suits, but still with brilliant red or green or blue sashes at the waist; and always handsome, black-haired women, with smooth olive skin over high cheekbones, walking proudly or standing with the men. Every

five-minute stop was a pageant especially arranged for
my northern eyes.

Things were just as good inside the coach. Just in
front of me were two young and tolerant parents, obviously on their way to a summer home in the south,
with two pretty little girls who were never still or
silent for a moment, yet never strident or annoying.
Across the aisle sat a huaso in full splendor, incongru-
ously guarding a small wicker suitcase. Two fine red-
headed girls were a few seats away, moving south on
some errand of pleasure, I hoped. And everyone was
relaxed and friendly, commenting on the heat, pulling
down shades, pushing up windows, hoping the train
would start and cool them off with a breeze, hoping it
would stop and let them shake off the cinders, which
were fewer and far less offensive than I had expected
from previous experience of riding in the open behind logging and freight locomotives. Probably the roof
helped.

Nearly everyone pulled out food and wine from time
to time, and I did quite well myself when I managed
to communicate with a white-coated waiter who pa-
trolled regularly through the car. He produced bottles
of good, cold beer at eight cents and a less good ham
sandwich at a slightly higher price, and even, when I
decided to vary the beer, a cup of sound, strong tea.
The country passed swiftly by. At Monte Aguila we
were in the pine forest whose eastern edges Mac and
I had skirted forty miles farther up the Laja. Near San
Rosendo the Laja joined the Bío Bío, after its drop
through the Salto del Laja. We passed among orchards
and olive groves, crossed broad rivers, stopped at little

towns, each with its plaza and church. An attractive honeymoon couple came aboard somewhere by the way, he looking like an English intellectual and reading an English literary periodical, she a pretty girl in any language, reading a German book; they spoke Spanish to each other. I was almost sorry when the hot coach pulled into Temuco exactly on time, and Jacko Edwards met me exactly as planned.

The Start of the South

JACKO EDWARDS IS A SANTIAGO NEWS-paperman, a keen trout fisherman and, like Frederico Weisner, a former member of the Chilean international tuna team. He is a slender, volatile man, a charming and extremely civilized companion. He is a true Chilean, but was born in England while his father was in the diplomatic service there and he was educated in Paris, returning to Chile when he was seventeen or eighteen. I spent the next month with Jacko, traveling the rivers and lakes of the south, from Temuco to Puerto Montt, and there wasn't a moment of him that I didn't enjoy.

Temuco is a town of some sixty thousand people, a clean and pretty place with some good stores and many things, including fishing tackle, camera film and Scotch whisky, which a tourist cannot always find readily in the south. I had all the tackle I needed; I am not a camera enthusiast and I had no intention of drinking whisky, Scotch or otherwise, in a country that produces a respectable gin, several good brandies, another admirable distillate of the grape called Pisco, and wines that are unequaled except in France. But I record the availability of these commodities out of respect for the good people of Temuco, and to counteract the arrogant assumption that, away from Santiago, shopping facilities in Chile are primitive. They are not. Osorno and Puerto Varas, and for all I know a dozen other places, are as much on the job as Temuco.

Temuco does, I think, still pride itself on being a frontier town—the name of its excellent, extremely modern hotel, Hotel de la Frontera, suggests that. It is the start of the south—the vegetation along the nearby rivers confirms that. And it is the heart of the Indian country, the land of the Araucanas, the proud race which never accepted conquest by the Spaniards. I say the heart of their country because Pedro Valdivia, the founder of Chile, is said to have been killed by the Indians on a rock bluff overlooking the Laja right by the Palacio, two hundred miles north of Temuco; because the last great war was fought around Villarica, fifty or sixty miles south; and because I saw more full-blooded Indians near Temuco than anywhere else. But in truth there has been in Chile such a magnificent freedom of intermarriage between the native Indians and the invading whites that it can be said the country is fairly apportioned between invaders and invaded, to the lasting benefit of both.

Jacko had already made arrangements to go fishing. After fourteen-hour days on the Laja and at Maule, they shocked me a little, but we were out of our com-

fortable beds by 4:30 the next morning and starting
from the hotel entrance in a rackety truck by 5:00
A.M. The truck carried two fair-sized hardwood skiffs,
ourselves, two boatmen, a driver and a swamper, whose
sole business was to help unload the heavy boats.

We jolted along some fifteen or twenty miles of
rough road to a bridge over the Cautin River, backed
the truck down as near to the water as possible and
slid the boats in, not without difficulty. The driver, a
keen fisherman himself, wished us good fishing, the
truck pulled away and we started out into the stream.

My boatman, Gemán Fonfach, was a very dignified,
respectable, middle-aged man, powerfully built and with
the obvious confidence of experience. He was reputed
to be the best boatman in the Temuco area, an enthusiast for the fly and himself both a good fisherman and
a good fly-tier. He took me firmly in hand at once,
which was reasonable enough, looked over my fly boxes
and indicated very pronounced preference for large flies
of an olive or yellowish brown type; his favorite was
the Norton, which seems to me a very large stone fly
imitation, and after that a big green drake or else the San
Pedro streamer, which is winged with long, barred
cock's hackles dyed yellow. He would have none of
Mac's Gray Ghost, which had done well for us on the
Laja, or of a brown shrimp fly that had risen me some
good fish. But he did let me use a fly of my own, dressed
with green gantron chenille and a mixed polar bear wing,
in a somewhat smaller size than his favorites.

All this interested me very much indeed, because I
knew I should be fishing with boatmen through much
of Chile and I was at least as anxious to learn about the

boatmen themselves as anything else. If one must have a guide, the manner of his guiding is all important to the day's pleasure. Choice of fly usually does not worry me too much, especially when I am fishing wet, and I make it a rule to fish a boatman's preference rather than my own whenever I reasonably can—it gives him confidence and encourages him to make more important concessions; besides, he may have some special knowledge. Fonfach, as it turned out, had.

He understood at once that I wanted to wade and cast wherever possible, but the first reaches of the Cautin offered little opportunity for this and he handled the boat beautifully through them while I cast into the likely places. We caught one or two small rainbows of a pound or so, then I rolled a good fish at the head of a deep run. "El flojo," Fonfach said. "The lazy one. Brown trout."

The river was easy and swift, over a gravelly bottom and through flat land; it is smaller than the Laja, it does not divide, as the Laja does, into many river-size branches, and the vegetation along its banks is generally richer and greener and stronger; yet the two rivers are somewhat similar and I could well believe in the Cautin's reputation as a great trout stream. But I could sense that Fonfach did not expect a big day. When I rolled a second big brown trout he was obviously surprised to see the fish, and just as obviously was not surprised when the fly came away. He explained why almost at once: November and December were the river's good months; January and February were too warm; all the big fish were lying deep and disinclined to take, though they would be moving again in March and April. I checked the river temperature and found it was 69° F.

As the stream opened up to shallower water Fonfach began to put me out at many favorable places, and I worked them comfortably and happily in the bright sunshine, finding an abundance of bright fourteen- and fifteen-inch rainbows, but nothing of any size. From time to time we passed and repassed Jacko and his boatman, and it was plain that Jacko, using a light spinning outfit with an assortment of plugs and spinners, was faring much as we were—no better, no worse. So I came to the time and place of my first real fishing lunch in Chile.

I had heard of these magnificent meals, but I was by no means prepared for the formality or the efficiency of the affair. We stopped opposite a wide, shallow reach of the river, where there were some fine trees and a heavy growth of bamboo. Almost immediately the two boatmen had a great fire of bamboo and hardwood burning strongly. Four bottles of wine were set in the river to cool. Jacko's boatman was cleaning and filleting some of the trout we had caught; Fonfach was preparing a long bamboo stake on which he impaled several pounds of mutton, to be barbecued when the fire had died down. It was clear that there was nothing for Jacko and me to do except lie in the shade and take our ease, and that, Jacko assured me, was exactly what we were expected to do.

"The boatmen will rest afterward," he said. "And for quite long enough. It is noon now. They will not start fishing again until three o'clock at the soonest."

"That's quite a while," I said. "What do they do?"

"Eat all the food and drink all the wine, then sleep. They say it is the bad hour for fish, from twelve till three, and nothing can be caught. But I don't see how they can know, because no one in Chile ever fishes at that time."

There were plates in front of us now, with fillets of trout swimming in black butter, another plate with an excellent salad of lettuce and tomatoes, hot green peppers and French dressing. The wine bottles were open. Fonfach had his meat browning over the fire, potatoes baking in the ashes, water boiling for coffee. I accepted the bad hour and was grateful for it.

Later, when the food was eaten and most of the wine was gone, I suppose I slept for a little. But I was awake at 1:30, listening to the chatter of parakeets in the trees above me. I could see them, none too clearly, against the sky, then suddenly the whole flock took off. They were brilliant green in the sunlight, slender bodies on narrow wings, like arrows, straight and swift in flight. I sat up and saw Jacko asleep on his back, the two boatmen asleep with their blanket ponchos thrown over them. I picked up my rod and stole away to the river.

It was an easy place to wade and I found a good run on the shady side of an island, within fifty yards of the boats. My pale green fly was taken solidly at the first cast and the fish ran hard, well down into the backing. Then he jumped and I was surprised to see a silvery rainbow not much larger than those I had been catching in the morning. I netted him and quickly took two others from the run, both excellent fighters

and exactly the same size as the first—sixteen inches and
one and three-quarters pounds.

I had noticed some very pale green caterpillars on
the bushes near where we had lunch and the quick
success of my green-bodied fly made me curious, so I
cleaned the fish at once. The caterpillars were in them,
with a few apancora and another pale green, shield-
shaped bug that Fonfach later called the sanfoin or
copiala beetle. I understood why my green-bodied fly
had taken his fancy.

It turned out that those three fish were the best of
the day, though Jacko and I killed twenty-five or thirty
between us, all of them over a pound. We ran through
some fine-looking water during the afternoon, passed
the boats over an irrigation dam a few miles above
Temuco and from there to the outskirts of the town
itself saw a dozen places that must hold big trout. I
was hopeful of the good hour between sunset and dark,
but we came to the end of the run before that—among
a multitude of the good citizens of Temuco swimming
in their warm stream and with a welcome from the
local fishing club, whose boats Fonfach had borrowed
for us.

It was, I suppose, a disappointing day, because the
Cautin has a considerable reputation for big fish. But
Fonfach assured me the reputation is well deserved; in
November and December one can expect an average
weight of two and a quarter pounds on most days,
with several fish of between four and six pounds. I
have little doubt he is right because a random sample
of our catch that day proved to be all fish in their
second or third year, none had spawned and most were

immature. A fourth-year fish would certainly be over two pounds and could be very much larger.

Our next day's fishing was in the Quepe, some twenty miles south of the Cautin and a very different stream. The Quepe is smaller than the Cautin, with brownish, rushing water, and it twists and turns its way between canyon-like clay banks that are often a hundred and fifty or two hundred feet high.

We started out cheerfully in the truck with the boats at some much too early hour, and pounded five or six miles over bad roads before discovering we had forgotten the lunch. Clearly the truck had to go back for it, and Jacko and I decided to walk until it caught up with us again. We were in rolling, rather dry country with a few primitive-looking thatched Indian huts scattered through it. Most of the huts had gardens, whose main crop seemed to be healthy-looking potatoes. We met many Indian women walking toward the town, some young, some old, all walking well and handsomely dressed in flowered dresses and dark blue capes of blanket-like material, often lined with red. They wore impressively heavy silver ornaments on their breasts, hinged and pieced, decorated with crosses and coins and sometimes beads. The workmanship was quite remarkable and the designs varied considerably; I felt they must have some significance, but our happy truck driver insisted they were simply decoration. I asked Jacko why we saw only women. "Only the women work," he said. "They are going to market to sell the stuff we have seen in the carts."

Our truck caught up to us, we climbed aboard and went on again. The driver was regretful he could not fish with us. The Quepe was his favorite river and we would surely have great sport. As we launched the boats he gave me, with Fonfach's approval, two big dark streamer flies he had tied himself on No. 2 hooks, each with a smaller hook trailing behind it. They were, he assured me, the best possible medicine for the river and as Fonfach seemed to agree I started out with the smaller one, a mixture of black and barred hackles.

The Quepe seemed to take us into herself almost immediately and we were lost between the high banks as though in a forest. The banks themselves were quite wonderful, dripping with fuchsia in full bloom, matted with bamboo, patterned with some lovely yellow flower almost like a pansy. Acacias and weeping willows and other handsome trees grew wherever there was root hold. The enormous leaves of the Giant Gunnera, often five or six feet across, stood out as a perpetual reminder of strangeness. And the river itself butted against the base of its banks, twisted round right-angled corners and broke white against log jams, in test after formidable test of Fonfach's skill with the boat. It was far from being the swiftest or fiercest of the boat rivers I saw in Chile, but in many ways it was the tightest and trickiest to work and I began to appreciate the skill and boldness that Chilean boatmen have.

It was a cloudy day and considerably cooler than any other day I had seen in Chile. The river temperature where we started in was only 60° F and I began to believe we should have a good day. We did. By lunchtime I had five fish of over two and a half pounds, the biggest a rainbow of just under four pounds, all of them caught on the truck driver's black streamer. There was a shower of rain at lunchtime, short and swift and violent, and when we began fishing again I noticed that fish were coming short to the streamer, so I changed again to my green fly—the only smallish fly I had that Fonfach would approve.

Most of the pools in this part of the Quepe are deep and dark, quite narrow and quite short, with a heavy run of water through them. At the head of a pool of this sort the green fly caught me a lovely four and a half pound brown trout. Soon after that I asked Fonfach to stop and let me work a pool where a narrow, two-hundred-foot fall poured straight down past a solid bank of blooming fuchsia. Another four-pound brown lay just past the foot of the fall and took the fly in a swirl of bronze. Neither of these fish rated Fonfach's contemptuous nickname, El Flojo, but later in the day, in a wider pool, I hooked a three-pound brown that walked clear across the current on his tail, for all the world like a marlin. I glanced at Fonfach and asked him, "El Flojo?" He laughed and shook his head. "Not always."

The truck met us at dusk by a bridge far down the river. I had returned over twenty fish, but Fonfach had kept smaller fish than I wanted and there were seventeen in the boat when we landed, eleven of them between two and a half and four and a half pounds. Jacko had a similar catch on spoon and flatfish though his best fish, to my surprise, was a three-pounder. As nearly as I could judge from the reactions of the boatmen and the truck driver and his helpers, the catch was a good one for the river at any time. Scale readings confirmed this, as the big brown trout were five-year-olds that had spawned previously and the best rainbow, a fish of three and three-quarters pounds, had spawned at three years. I thought it a fine day, though I should have been content to fish only a quarter of the distance in the same length of time. We had passed dozens of wonderful places without fishing them, and it seemed to me we had come to the best water very late in the day.

No small part of the pleasure of a Chilean day like this is in the sharp contrast between the wildness of the river and its surroundings and the luxury of the evening at the hotel. By ten-thirty we had changed our clothes, had a quiet drink in the bar and were sitting down to dinner in the big, graceful dining room of the Frontera. There was good food, well served, and good wine to go with it. A small orchestra played South American music at the far end of the room. Well-dressed men and handsome women sat at the other tables around the room; faded blue denims and Hawaiian sports shirts, weather-ravaged faces and casual manners simply were not to be seen. At seven or seven-thirty all this would have been an intolerable nuisance, to be avoided by any sensible fisherman. But at ten-thirty or eleven, the day is over, the last hour has been fished, daylight is exhausted. It is a perfect time to relax, to enjoy an appetite and feel thoroughly civilized.

The Tolten

Our next river was the Tolten, fifty or sixty miles south of Temuco and perhaps the most beautiful and best-known river in Chile. The river is said to be overfished, but I seriously doubt that. There are thirty or more miles of good fishing water between Lake Villarica and the mouth of the Alli-pen, usually covered in three separate days by boat, from the lake to Prado Verde, from Prado Verde to Catrico

74

and Catrico to Alli-pen. I have heard there are as many as twenty boats a day spread through this thirty miles, but even when this is so I do not think it would represent very intensive fishing. There were other boats out on the days I fished, some of them traveling through the whole thirty miles in one trip, all of them going too far and passing much good water. Very few Chilean fishermen indeed stop their boats and get out and wade, which means that the heads of nearly all the pools are left unfished, because boats cannot be held in place to cover them properly. Given satisfactory spawning seasons I should think the river could support several times the fishery it now has.

But the Tolten below Prado Verde, or rather below the mouth of the Carrileufu, suffered severely in the disastrous eruption of the volcano Villarica in January of 1949. The eruption melted the glaciers and poured floods of hot, silt-laden water down the watercourses. The settling basin of Villarica Lake protected the upper reaches of the Tolten, but the Carrileufu runs directly from the volcano into the river and its fierce, hot flood must have destroyed everything for many miles below. The records at Catrico show that as many as forty fish a year of five pounds and over were taken from this part of the river up until 1949. In the 1949-50 season there was no five-pounder. In the 1950-51, there was one. In 1951-52, the season I fished there, five-pounders began to show up again. Horace Graham, Jr., had killed a lovely seven-pound rainbow the day I arrived, which proved to be a five-year-old and so had probably moved up or down the river. All the other fish I saw from below the Carrileufu were two- and

three-year-olds except one four and a half pound brown
trout, which was a four-year-old. Yet in one day's fishing on the upper river I had several four-year-old fish.

The Tolten is a big, clear, blue-green river, fast but
with deep swirling pools under high steep banks and
plenty of broken water where one can get out of the
boat to wade and cast. I fished the two lower reaches
of the river from Catrico, the summer home of Horace
Graham, who is one of the authentic giants of South
America and the most perfect host a fisherman could
wish for. Horace Graham is first and foremost a mining engineer, a graduate of Columbia University who
worked in the Western United States, then found his
way to Bolivia. In Bolivia he lived hard—it is a hard
country—and specialized in getting things done. From
there he found Chile and the great nitrate deposits. For
a modern empire builder he is a shockingly modest man.
"I don't really know how it happened," he told me.
"It just does. You get in there somehow and can't seem
to stop. I know lots of good mining engineers, in the
west, in Bolivia, all through South America, better men
than I am. Most of them never got into it, that's all."
I feel pretty sure that is the most disarming success
story I shall ever hear.

Unfortunately, Horace Graham couldn't get out on
the river during the days I was there, but his son and
daughter-in-law came with me from Prado Verde to
Catrico, and Horace, Jr., came with me again the next
day, from Catrico to Alli-pen. I remember those days
in impressions rather than in detail, perhaps chiefly because I was so fascinated by the beauty of the river
and all that went on about me.

On the first day we seemed to be lost, almost from the start, between green-forested walls that went straight up from the broad river. The growth was far heavier than along the banks of the Cautin and the Quepe and its greens were impressively rich. Bird song was constant when one could hear above the sound of the river, and at one place bandurrias scolded and complained from the high treetops about our passing. Wherever cut-banks prevented the growth of vegetation I saw the little South American churretes, much like our streamside dippers and with the same abrupt little motions, though a more slender body shape and a white stripe over the eye made me hesitate about identification. Many had nests where high water had eaten holes into the banks.

Of all the birds of Chile, the one I most wanted to see was the torrent duck, or correntino as he is locally called. I have long admired our own North American mergansers as superb divers and swimmers, masters of swift water and admirable companions of the river. I first discovered the torrent ducks in Peter Scott's *Key to the Wildfowl of the World* and I was immediately impressed by their name and their slender, streamlined shape, plainly even better adapted to swift water than that of the merganser. But I understood from the books that one must look for them in "the mountain torrents of the high Andes," and this the Tolten, for all its broken swiftness, plainly was not. Yet it was on the Tolten, on my first morning on the river, that I saw them.

There were five: drake, duck and three young ones, sitting on a log six or eight feet above a run of swift water. They did not fly at the approach of the boat, but dove straight down to the water, disappeared momentarily, then swam on, a compact little group, apparently without fear but not without reasonable caution. I turned to Tilo Aiado, my boatman, for confirmation. "Correntinos?" I asked.

Tilo nodded and, seeing my interest, kept the boat as close as he could without worrying them. I was surprised by their colors, for I had not expected much brightness, only graceful form and water skill. The male's head and back were crisply patterned in black and white, his beak was bright scarlet; there was green in his wing and red on his belly. The female was a grayish, quiet-looking duck until one saw the brilliant scarlet of her breast and belly; it was a live color, glowing and rich as the ruby red of the harlequin's flank. These were added pleasures, but to have seen the ducks only a year or two after I had first known of them and felt the strong desire to see them was a pleasure that needed no embellishment.

When we stopped for lunch Horace and I had done none too well—I think our best fish were rainbows of about two pounds—but Mrs. Graham had a fine brown trout of over four pounds and several others up to three. We stopped for lunch at a grassy flat fifteen or twenty feet above the river and surrounded by great trees. I noticed a scarlet-flowered vine and asked if it were Chile's national flower, the Copihue. It was not; the Copihue (Lapageria rosea), as I found later, is much larger, with waxy, crimson, bell-shaped flowers that make it one of the handsomest of all climbing plants. But from that we began talking of Chile. I was concerned about the gentle, half-humorous complaint I had heard again and again that Chileans are lazy and inefficient. I knew that the Grahams lived and worked at the nitrate mines and I felt they would have a sound opinion.

"They don't seem lazy to me," I said. "Or inefficient. Look at Tilo. He's worked like a slave for me all morning with that heavy boat in difficult water. He's got great horny calluses that stand up half an inch from his hands. Fonfach was the same. They work harder than Canadians or Americans and they're really good with a boat. How are they in the mines?"

"They're good people," Horace said. "You can teach them anything. Up north it is very dry and they have to stop pretty often to drink something or they'd be desiccated. They drink tea, and we pay people to do nothing else but make fires and keep water boiling for tea, but that is necessary."

Wages are good in the mines; two and a half or three dollars a day, compared with the fifty-cent wage of the agricultural worker of central Chile. "What about machinery?" I asked. "Can they handle it and look after it? People say they can't."

"They have to learn," Horace said. "But they can learn. We had a big new concrete mixer come in the other day. Took me a week to get on to it myself, then I taught one of the men to handle it and within a week he was turning out more than the rated capacity of the machine. Looking after it, too."

"Then they could do the same with farm machinery?"

"Sure. It's farm people that come up to work with us most of the time. We have to keep wages down so as not to dislocate the whole economy of the country. But we make it up by selling far below cost in all the commissaries."

We talked also of the wonderful deep-sea fishing in the Humboldt current, off Tocapilla and Iquique, where broadbills of four to eight hundred pounds are almost common—not suspecting then that a fifteen-hundred-pound black marlin would come from Cabo Blanco, a little farther north, only eighteen months later. So the quiet, hot midday hours passed until it was time to go on down the lovely river again.

The next day Horace and I went down over the lowest reach, to the mouth of the Alli-pen. The way was through flatter, more open country and the river was wider and shallower, broken by little islands and gravel bars. There was a high hot sun and a strong wind, but we fished hard and by noon had five fish each, up to three pounds or a little over. The water temperature was 68° F at noon, four degrees higher than it had been farther upstream at the same time the previous day. This, with the effect of the eruption of 1949, convinced me that this part of the river must offer magnificent fly fishing in the early and late months of the season, when water temperatures should be down in the fifties. Off the mouth of the Alli-pen, whose cold flow cut the river back to 63° F, Horace took the best fish of the day late in the evening. But the Alli-pen is a glacial stream, heavy with silt, and I understand there is little good fishing below it.

I left Catrico and the Grahams, very regretfully, the next day, to rejoin Jacko Edwards at the Hotel Yachting, a small and pleasant chalet at the foot of Villarica

Lake. Tilo Aiado was there to meet me and continue
fishing with me, and that evening we went out to work
the bar, where the river drops out of the lake.

A great deal of bar fishing is done in Chile—at Villarica, Pucon, Llifen, Puerto Nuevo, Petrohue, wherever the big rivers enter or leave the lakes. I avoided
it for the most part, because it is sedentary fishing, and
it was easy enough to check on its yield by the catches
other fishermen brought to the hotels. But it is, just
the same, a pleasant and satisfying occupation. The fish
collect well at these places, especially in the evening
and early morning, and they are likely to be both big
and on the feed.

Tilo and I had a lovely evening on the bar of the
Tolten. I made him take me up the lake first, so that
I could get temperature readings at various depths and
a plankton sample. Tilo was both fascinated and confused—confused by anyone who would stop fishing for
such affairs, fascinated by the moving rotifers and flag-
ellates and crustaceans I showed him in my plankton
catch.

The water was glassy and lovely, pulling down into
the river's first rapid as we came to the bar in the evening light. It was all pleasant and lazy, in the clear
tradition of Chilean fishing, and I was glad to be part
of it for once. Behind us the hills built superbly from
the edge of the lake to the white cone of the volcano,
and the day's volcanic smoke collected the red of the
setting sun all along the sky. Tilo held the boat in
the smooth, strong pull of the current, I let the fly
hang deep and a slim, three-pound race horse of a fish
tore at it and jumped instantly into the red light. As

he netted her, Tilo said, "From the lake." He dropped the boat down a little and I threw behind an exposed rock in the rapid. A short, thick fish took there, bright as the other, just as heavy and just as strong. Netting this one, Tilo said, "From the river." I wondered how he knew and if he really knew.

It was very peaceful and lovely there by the little town along the lake's edge. The lights were on in the houses as we rowed back toward the hotel and as the boats came to the wharf the last star of the Southern Cross was bright in the southern sky.

During dinner, Jacko said, "Tomorrow you must make a very big catch."

"Why?" I asked.

"There have not been big catches lately, and Tilo wants it."

"Tilo is all right," I said. "He's a first-class boatman. We'll catch some fish, but we won't break any records with the river up around 64° or 65°."

"It is important to Tilo," Jacko told me. "He says, 'the caballero can wade up to his neck and cast across the river. It is a pleasure to fish with him because he knows so well everything that will happen before it does happen. But I have not caught a lot of fish for him.'"

I knew how Tilo felt and I resolved to fish hard for him as we started down the river next day. Tilo is a short, dark, wiry man of about thirty, with a small, neat mustache and rather anxious eyes. He is very strong, brave on the water, quick as a cat, proud as nearly all Chileans are, yet quiet and intense about it rather than bold and reckless. I had liked him from

the start and in three days had begun to feel very close
to him, though we could talk little.

It was a brilliant sunny day with a cool upstream
breeze. We started well, with a nice fish of two and
a half pounds just below the bar and a better one that
threw the fly after a long run and one jump just below. For some reason I had checked my watch at each
of these incidents, and I pulled an envelope out of my
pocket and noted them on the back of it. I had never
thought of doing such a thing before, but I decided I
would keep track of everything that happened between
me and the fish throughout the day. In the next hour
I missed several rises, lost at least one good fish, killed
one or two of about fourteen inches "for lunch" and
returned others still smaller. Right after that, from ten-
twenty till eleven-twenty we had a completely blank
hour.

The river was much as it had been between Prado
Verde and Catrico, deep and strong and broken, between high green banks. There were not many places
where Tilo could put me out to fish from my feet,
but he was clever at finding long runs close under the
banks, where he could hold the boat toward the center of the river and let me fish accurately down. I had
three fine fish, one of three pounds and two just under, from a run of this type, fishing into the shade
from the sunlight. A little farther down he found a
run where I could wade; I killed two strong, bright
two-pounders from it and returned three smaller fish.
From there we ran on down to join the others for
lunch, at about twelve-thirty.

It was a long, luxurious lunch, lasting until three-

forty-five. Four other boats had left the lake at about
the same time as ourselves, but I had seen little of
them during the morning and little of Jacko. He was
waiting at the lunch place with a young, handsome
Chilean from Santiago, Señor Castano. The other three
boats, Jacko's boatman said, had gone on down—they
were making the run through to Catrico. I thought
they would have little time to fish, and this seemed
to be the case because they came in at the end of the
day with very little to show for themselves. Jacko and
Señor Castano had not done too well either, so Tilo
was well satisfied with our catch of half a dozen bright
rainbows, all of them over two pounds.

Trout, a quarter of lamb, fresh peas and peaches and
a rich, red Concha y Toro of 1942 made our lunch.
Tilo cut himself while preparing the lamb and at once
became very excited; he hurled the knife into the
ground, swore at it, jumped up and down, swore much
more, then grabbed salt and piled it on the cut while
we all sympathized. It was a very small cut and did
not bleed very much. I think he was religiously afraid
of the blood, as though it were some insult or per-
manent loss to his body; yet moments later he was
laughing and happy again.

We lay back in the shade of a great, aromatic Boldo
tree and talked of Chile's blessed freedom from biting
insects. There are no poisonous snakes, either, Jacko
boasted. But there are tarantulas and scorpions, Señor
Castano suggested. Yes, Jacko agreed, but very few
and they do not bite seriously. I knew this would be
true in a temperate climate, but we asked Tilo and the
other boatmen if they had seen scorpions. They had

not, but had heard of them. I asked if they knew of
the litre, a poisonous tree that grows around the Laja.
They had not, and I did not see the tree again in Chile,
so perhaps the southern climate is not favorable to it.

I was half-asleep, watching the sunlight on the leaves
of the tree, when I heard Jacko and Señor Castano
discussing women and fidelity.

Castano asked me, "In Canada they expect you to
have only one and to be loyal?"

I said that was the general idea, though by no means
rigidly observed.

Castano shook his head solemnly. "Here it is different. You must not flaunt it in front of your wife, but
she expects it. Not another one much, or all the time,
but for a little while, for a week."

He seemed a little distressed, so I pointed out again
that I was not claiming rigid observance of the de-
sired standards by my countrymen.

"That is true," he agreed more cheerfully. "There
are many divorces, are there not? But in Chile, it is
different. The people are very active sexually. It is the
climate and the wine and the food, especially the peppers and all the sea food."

After lunch Tilo and I left a little behind the other
boats and I was glad of a long, fierce-looking but not
really fierce rapid to work out some of the courage
of the wine. There were a few big rocks, with shade
and slackening under the far bank. But no fish. "They
are later than we are," I told Tilo, and he laughed.

A small flock of the little parrots flew calling across
the river. Two eagles were perched on a high cliff at
the end of the long reach and a queltegue scolded them.

We slid around a bend in the river and Tilo said suddenly, "El Volcan."

I looked back and saw it straight up the river, serene and white and beautiful. I could tell from Tilo's voice how important a thing it was to him. "There is no smoke," I said.

"Tomorrow there will be," Tilo told me. And then the fish began to move again.

Tilo put me out to wade a lovely run and I was into a fine fish right away. He ran me fifty or sixty yards, then the fly came free in the bright water. Farther down, in a stretch of difficult wading and long casting, I killed a two-and-a-half-pounder and lost a two-pounder at the net. We both laughed happily over the loss.

Back in the boat again Tilo worked some good water very carefully and I was with him all the way, guiding the fly into the places where the fish must be and holding it there as long as possible with just the work on it Tilo likes. A fish pulled at me and we both thought him a good one, but he would not come again. Then a three-and-a-half-pound brown took solidly. It was in bad water and she did well for a brown, but our real joy was in her shape and color. She was pale for a brown, with tail and dorsal fin heavily spotted with black; her platinum belly was clean and bright and all over her sides were great dark markings rather than spots, with an iridescent turquoise color in them, while a few had a touch of red as though the ordinarily varied spots of a brown trout had been blended. She was undoubtedly the most beautifully colored trout

I have ever caught and perfectly shaped, a maiden three-year-old, nineteen inches long.

About an hour later I hooked the best fish of the day. I was fishing a short, streamy run, very fast, close under the shade of the south bank and full of snags. Tilo was waiting just behind me with the boat. The fish took deep and very hard. Tilo said behind me, "Quick. Get in." A moment later we were sliding down the center of the river and I was guiding the fish behind us, away from the snags and dangers of his favorite lie.

Tilo ran the boat down for two or three hundred yards to a quiet bay under the far bank. The fish was still strong and fought with short heavy rushes and jarring head shakes, but Tilo netted him at last—no monster but a handsome, golden-bronze brown trout of four and a half pounds.

According to my tattered envelope, this was at six-forty-five. We tried hard for the next two hours, until we came to Prado Verde Grande at the end of the run. I lost one good fish and pulled another by Prado Verde Chico. A three-pounder took firmly and came to the net just below and something really big grabbed the fly and instantly released it in a swirl of deep currents under a mud bank. After that there were one or two small fish, but nothing worth keeping.

At Prado Verde Grande a horse and cart were waiting to pull the heavy boats up the steep hill to the meadow. We took off our waders at the water's edge while Tilo and the other boatmen checked over the catch. I was afraid Tilo would be disappointed because we had nothing really big, not even a five-pounder to top off the catch. But it was evident, as we walked slowly up behind the horse and wagon, that he was a thoroughly happy man. "He is very proud," Jacko told me. "They are saying it is the best catch there has been for a long while, twelve fish all between one and two kilos, and on the fly."

The taxi was very late in picking us up and it was quickly cold with the sun gone, so the boatmen built an enormous fire in the meadow. I sat beside it and checked the jottings on my envelope. We had fished just under eight hours to kill twelve fish and release eight or nine others. But counting missed rises and lost fish there had been a total of nearly forty incidents between me and the fish that day, an average of just under five per hour. I didn't feel much wiser for the information, but I was surprised there had not been more than this, because the day had seemed so intensely full and active.

The taxi came at last and the boatmen had a tremendous time to put the fire out. They beat it and battered it and pulled apart and were inclined to leave it at that, but my northern conscience couldn't stand it so we all dragged up and down the steep hill with pots and pans and hats full of water until it was truly out. Like nearly everything else, this was a wonderful joke, full of laughter for everyone. We piled somehow into the taxi, fish, tackle, lunch baskets and everyone, and laughed all through the jolting ride back to the hotel.

The White Water of Liucura and Trancura

 $\mathbf{F}$ ROM VILLARICA IT IS ALMOST INEVI-
table to go to Pucon, a journey of only fifteen or
twenty miles along the south shore of the lake, under
the foot of the volcano and across the torn wastes of
its minor watercourses. It is almost as inevitable to go
to the Gran Hotel Pucon, one of half a dozen or more
first-class hotels built here and there about southern
Chile by the government railroad to encourage tourist
travel. The hotel at Pucon has just about every luxury
the heart could desire, from terraced pools and foun-
tains to bars and barber shops and a magnificent dining room. It is too luxurious, I suppose, for simple fly
fishermen, and certainly it attracts visitors of many
other types—swimmers and yachtsmen, horsemen, climb-
ers, golfers and just plain vacationers. But it treats the
fisherman with every possible concern, welcomes his
early goings and late comings, arranges for transportation and boatmen, looks after his fish, puts up his
lunches and generally recognizes him as a civilized and
rational member of society.

Most fishermen who stay at Pucon are devotees of
the barra, where the Trancura River enters Villarica
Lake by several mouths and the rainbow trout come in
to feed at dawn and dusk. This is fine fishing, but there

is fine fishing up the rivers, too, and some of the most exciting water one is likely to run over in the course of an ordinary lifetime. There are one or two awe-inspiring rapids on the Tolten and there are many fierce and tricky places on the Quepe, but the Grahams had told me these were as nothing compared to the white water of the Trancura and its tributary, Liucura, and they had spoken with unstinted admiration of the boatmen who run these rivers, especially of the brothers Zapata.

My boatman was Eleazar Zapata, a handsome, splendidly built man of about thirty. Of all the brothers, he is considered the specialist in fly fishing, and I think perhaps he may be the boldest of them all in running the rivers, though that is presuming a lot since I have not traveled with the others. Certainly Eleazar has a fine bold approach to his work, a genuine love of fierce water and all the superb confidence in his own strength and skill that makes a river virtuoso. It would not be too much to say Eleazar is boastful on occasion—but he boasts as a Zapata, which is to say as one of the elite who cannot really boast. It might not be too much to say he can be reckless, but it is a recklessness within his powers, born of his own skill and sheer joy in his rivers.

We started out quite early on the morning after we arrived at Pucon, four of us with a driver crammed into a 1931 Ford touring car. The boats had gone on through to Liucura bridge by oxcart the previous evening. Our way through the village was triumphal; everyone seemed to realize that here were Zapatas going fishing, and everyone had a shout or a wave for us, including the proudest horsemen and the prettiest girls. But soon we were out of the village and off on a rutted cart track along which the Ford purred smoothly and sweetly, climbing the steepest rises in unfailing high gear.

We traveled a considerable distance in this way, crossing the Upper Trancura by a fairly good bridge, occasionally passing wagons drawn by oxen or horses, but meeting nothing. I wondered many times what would happen if we did meet something. Just short of Liucura bridge, on a twisting downgrade, we met something— an oxcart lumbering upwards, filling the whole road. Without the slightest hesitation our driver swung off, plowed into a briar patch and came up with a fairly solid jolt against a big log. Everyone laughed heartily and there was some fairly excited talk which Jacko interpreted for me very simply: "He has no brakes."

As soon as the oxcart was past, the driver started the Ford again, backed out of the briar patch and continued with undiminished speed to Liucura bridge. We piled out, launched the boats and started down.

The Liucura at this point is quite small and I began to wonder how it would maintain its fierce reputation. True, it was fast and in places very awkward between the great trunks of fallen trees. But there wasn't a two-foot current wave anywhere, nor weight of water to make one. I caught one or two small fish, and in a little while we came to the mouth of the Carguello, a clear cold stream from Caburga Lake, which carries almost as much water as the Liucura itself and enters at a magnificent pool of cross currents and turbulent depths. It is a natural place for big fish, perhaps for a monster, and we spent some time searching it thoroughly and faithfully. I checked the temperature and found it 50° F, two degrees colder than the Liucura and ten degrees colder than any stream I had checked except the mountain torrents flowing down to Maule Lake. I began to think we should have a good day.

Looking down into the swirling depths of clear water, I saw the shadowy substance of a five- or six-pounder. We tried for him with the fly, letting it wash far down under the surface and swirl with the currents, but there was no way of telling whether it ever came within his sight. Jacko searched the pool with a flatfish and again with a spoon. But in the end we had to go on, having moved nothing bigger than fourteen or fifteen inches.

From there down the river was altogether bigger and stronger, with many fine deep pools, their bottoms littered with flood-borne limbs and hardwood trunks, for most of the trees of the Chilean rain forest are heavier than water. I fished with care and concentration, but cannot remember that I stirred a decent fish, though there undoubtedly were good fish all through the reach. Jacko fished hard, too, and at one point his flatfish, or caiman, as Eleazar called it, hooked what seemed like a really big trout. It ran hard downstream for sixty or seventy yards without breaking at all, then we could see from our boat that it was a fish of about two and a half pounds, foul-hooked in the belly.

We stopped for lunch at a little tumbledown farm on the right bank of the stream. It was a pretty place, close under the hills and with a superb view of the volcano across the river. But Jacko told me at once, "This is not a usual place to stop for lunch. One of the Zapatas has business here—business or a woman. You will see. I will find out about it."

There was a flock of tame geese at the edge of the river and a few small pigs snorted and fussed near the boats. A small dark boy appeared, watching us in silent, happy curiosity; there are always small dark boys along rivers where fishermen go, including my own son along my home river in Canada, but they are just a little more certain to show up in Chile than anywhere else. Close behind him came an old gentleman with a beard. Then an oldish woman, gray-haired, wearing a woolen cap, quite spare and slender—she might have been a lady of the manor somewhere in rural England. Lastly, there came a younger woman of thirty-five or forty, quick, very brown, very confident and vigorous. She welcomed us gracefully and brought hot bread and home-made cheese, both very good—not for money, Jacko told me, but for courtesy and hospitality.

They left us quite soon, with serious, sincere smiles and courteous words, and Eufrasio Zapata, Jacko's boatman, went with them. I asked Jacko what we could do in return.

"Nothing," he said. "It is all right. You will see."

"It is a small farm," I said. "And not very rich land. There should be something we can do for them."

"You saw the young woman," Jacko said. "She is an Indian. They are very rich. They have two million pesos at least and they could live in Santiago if they wished. But they prefer this."

Soon a little shriveled old man with an iron-gray beard, riding a neat bay horse, came down to the far side of the river. Without hesitation the horse began to wade the river, picking his way, upstream or down, through the fast and difficult crossing so that he was never much more than belly deep. The old man sat gracefully in his sheepskin saddle, his head nodding a little to the horse's movement, but otherwise perfectly still and seemingly absorbed in his thoughts. As he came along the track toward us he saluted courteously, with great dignity, and said something in Spanish. We returned the salute and Eleazar said something in return. Everyone laughed and the old man went on to the farm.

"He is the padrone," Jacko told me.

"The father of the brown woman?" I asked.

"No, the husband. The father of the little boy. And it is business Eufrasio has at the house. He is trading his boat to them for pigs. Next season all the Zapatas will have new boats, all painted in the same colors."

I looked at Eufrasio's rather battered boat, patched here and there with tin. It wasn't in bad shape, but obviously it needed loving attention from time to time as the rapids of Liucura and Trancura worked it over. "How do they know it is a good boat?"

"They need a boat here," Jacko said. "This is a Zapata boat. But Eufrasio is a very smart dealer. He shows the boat now. It will grow older through the rest of the season. He chooses the pigs now. They will grow bigger while the boat grows older."

The sun was high and brilliant, the volcano shone white in the distance, a strong wind stirred the heavy leaves of the hardwood trees. We lay contentedly in the shade and drank the wine, too good and too much, that the hotel had put in with the lunches. Eleazar told

Jacko, "The meat was not good. The wine is good, but too expensive. For half the money I will bring the wine and lunch tomorrow and it will be better."

We came to the first bad rapid very soon after lunch. The river closed down into a bend, with great trees on either side; white water leapt and battered over rocks, reared into waves and burst into spray. Eleazar forced the boat with powerful oar strokes from side to side among the rocks; waves battered at the hardwood sides and occasionally broke clear over the stern; everything was turmoil and speed and roar of sound, and I could watch only the way we were going. I saw a pair of torrent ducks, through spray, sitting on a rock in the midst of the wildest water. They slid from it as the boat approached, disappeared in foam, found another rock fifty yards below, still in wild water, and flipped easily onto it. They stayed there calmly enough as we passed on the other side of the river, then flew as Eufrasio and Jacko approached, very low to the water, seeming to twist and turn their swift way among the waves. We came suddenly to a flat pool between low rock walls, a smooth swift current drawing through it and breaking white here and there on great square rocks near the surface. I had pulled the rods well inboard as we started down the rapid, so that there would be no risk of breaking their tips against a rock or in a heavy wave. Eleazar handed me one. "Casting," he said briefly.

Eleazar is a fly changer. He had explored my boxes thoroughly all through the morning and had handed me new flies to try at least half a dozen times. He had also made me scale down my leader from 9/5 to ix. So I found myself fishing a small streamer fly with a silver

body, a bushy squirreltail wing, blue hackle and tail
of yellow wool and tippets. How it had come into my
box I don't know, but it had caught me two nice fish
above the rapid and now it took, in swift succession,
lovely bright rainbows of two and three-quarters, three,
and four and a half pounds, all from that little, narrow,
rock-bound pool. They were strong fish and difficult
to handle, especially the four-pounder, but Eleazar netted them all quickly and skillfully. He was in a state
of high elation. "Pull in," he said, using the second of
his two English phrases. I reeled in, drew the rods back
out of harm's way and down we went into the next
rapid.

It was an afternoon of pure and sparkling action,
rapid after powerful rapid as the river rounded the
base of a great mountain, with now and then another
short, narrow pool that yielded a fish or two. There
was no doubt about the power and force of the river,
and no doubt at all about its difficulty. I wondered
again and again if I could have taken a sixteen-foot
Peterborough through safely, much less a heavy skiff.
The rapids were narrow, often no more than boat's-
width chutes between the rocks, and the rocks were
staggered so that from a few yards above there seemed
no way at all between them. Many were hidden, though
evident, from the upstream side by a flurry of white
water combing over them, yet plainly visible through
the spray from downstream. Occasionally we touched
a rock, always lightly, and occasionally waves sluiced
over and into my lap. But there was never a moment
when Eleazar wasn't in full control—not even when an
oarlock jumped from its socket or when he was pull-

ing his hardest to hold above a rock while getting in position to slide down past it. And all the while I could see in his face and movements the exuberant happiness I remember in the white water friends of my youth.

The country on both sides of the river, flat on the left bank, rising steeply to the mountains from the right bank, was wild and empty, with a heavy growth of young trees under the fire-killed frames of the original forest. The sound, and even the movement of the wind, was lost in the stream's wild movement. We turned and twisted with the river from brilliant sunlight into shade into sunlight again. Several times I saw torrent ducks closely, the black and white of the male's head, the glowing scarlet of the female's breast, and caught my breath in wonder at the fierceness of the water that seemed to delight them.

We came at last, in one of the river's wildest places, upon a rookery of black cormorants' nests in the trees above the left bank. There were young birds, almost full grown, in the nests, and the old birds, gleaming like black satin in the sunlight, were flying back and forth or perched precariously to feed their young. In spite of the sunlight and their own strange beauty and the loveliness of everything about me, I was somehow reminded of Shakespearean witches upon a blasted heath.

Just below the rookery we stopped on a rocky shore and waited for the others to catch up. I could see the sharp drop of tumbled water below us where Liucura joined the larger Trancura and was swept around a right-angled bend. Eleazar was studying the junction and seemed not to like it. Several times before I had noticed him signaling to Eufrasio the way down a particularly bad rapid and now, when Eufrasio arrived, he took him and explained carefully how he must bring his boat through. Jacko and I walked about a hundred yards to a point below the junction. "He says he would take you down," Jacko told me, "but it is better to go alone and show my boatman the way. I do not think he has been down before."

The boats came through as we watched, Eleazar easily and loving it, Eufrasio a little less sure, but competent enough. It did not seem to me as awkward as many other places we had passed, but there may have been something bad in the height of the water, because I ran it comfortably a month later with Eleazar and Riffo, another very experienced boatman.

We had come now to the long, broken reach of the Martinez Pool, and we found fish here and there all the way down it. The sun had gone before we reached the tail of the pool and suddenly fish were rising and jumping everywhere about us. I could plainly see a hatch of small May flies on the water and occasional sedges with them, but I hadn't a floating fly with me. I covered rise after rise with my wet fly; occasional fish came at it halfheartedly, but I think I only hooked two in all that wonderful rise. Nothing would touch Jacko's flatfish. Happily, this was the end of the run and we left the boats there, so I could promise myself I would come better prepared the next morning.

We had a walk of a mile or so along a dusty trail to a ferry. The first ferry, across a small arm of the river, was a skiff handled by a little boy who had just caught a two-pound rainbow on an enormous hook with an assortment of feathers tied to it. The second was one of the regular scow-shaped cable ferries, government-owned, that one finds on most of the rivers of Chile. We shared it with two oxcarts and several horses, and the Ford with no brakes met us at the other side.

Driving home through the dark, I was well satisfied. I had taken twenty fish, all rainbows (there are no browns in the Trancura or Liucura), weighing well over forty pounds, and had seen a river worth a lifetime's search with a boatman Neptune might have hired on a lucky day. The outline of the volcano was soft in the evening light and a line of Lombardy poplars stood bravely against the red light of the western sky. Each horseman we passed along the road seemed borne by a little traveling cloud of dust about his horse's feet.

When we came to the ferry again the next morning, it was in midstream, coming toward us. Several horsemen were aboard and as the ferry landed they mounted and clattered off. One girl did not. She was a very pretty girl of seventeen or eighteen, small and quick and graceful, full of laughter as she argued about something with the ferryman. Her horse carried a sidesaddle, with heavy saddlebags which Eleazar said were full of cheeses for the market. She wore a white shirt, open at the throat, a long, full skirt of pale blue denim and high-heeled patent leather pumps on which she frisked and whirled like a ballerina. She seemed to be scolding and laughing and on the verge of making love all at the same time, and all of it was pretty to watch.

"What's it all about?" I asked Jacko.

"She comes from a farm way up in the hills," he told me, pointing to a steep valley that ran back from the far side of the river. "They are very poor people, but every day she comes to the market with her cheeses and every day she must cross by the ferry. She wants the ferryman to help her on to her horse, but he says first he must have a cheese for all the times he has carried her on the ferry."

"I thought the ferry was free."

"It is," Jacko said. "But the ferryman is good to her. She will give him a cheese. You will see. But first she must tease a little and bargain a little."

As he spoke the ferryman stooped courteously, cupped his hand for her foot and with the lightest of movements she was in the saddle, settled there firmly and gracefully. Still laughing, she pulled a cheese from the saddlebag and tossed it to him with the air of a queen scattering largesse; then she flicked her horse with a little bamboo switch, clattered off the ferry and up to the wagon road without a backward glance. Some of the day's sparkle seemed to go with her.

At the Martinez Pool the fish were not rising as they had been the night before, but I waded in with a light rod and took a bright two-and-a-half-pounder on the first drift. There was a very strong wind and the wading was difficult, but I worked out as far as I could and took two more good fish quite quickly. This was the first time I had used the dry fly in Chile, though I had several times considered it before, especially on the Quepe, where there is a lot of favorable water. The constant search for big fish, the long boat-runs over strange water and the normal preference of the trout for crayfish over other feed are against it on the whole, but if one has time for it, and especially if one knows what to expect of the water, it can be a thoroughly effective method.

There was not too much time for experiment on this day, as we had a longish run before us and hoped to fish the Trancura bar in the evening, so I soon climbed into the boat with Eleazar, who was just as pleased as I was with the success of the dry fly.

He rowed out a little and put me within reach of a big rock where we had seen a good fish show. I drifted the fly over without response and let the float continue along the side of the rock. A very big fish came at it fiercely, but missed so plainly that I did not even strike. He would not come again, so I picked up the big rod and gave him the little streamer fly that had been successful the day before. He had it at once, in a great broad flash of silver right at the surface, and was away on a run that took him halfway across the wide pool —all the way, for all I know, because the fly came suddenly free. I looked at Eleazar's face of despair and could not help laughing.

"El Grande," I said. "Dos y media kilos."

He shook his head fiercely. "Tres," he said, pounding on the handle of his oar. "Tres, tres, tres kilos. Mas. Muy malo."

I think Eleazar was probably right; the fish was nearer seven pounds than five, but a fish that gets away always carries some insoluble secret with him.

We left the Martinez Pool soon after that and I was sad to leave it because it is, without a doubt, one of the truly great trout pools of the world. One could spend a whole day there or many days, and not begin to know it.

There are some fine pools and some magnificent rapids between the Martinez Pool and the ferry, but we fished with little effect through the morning. I think I had only two more fish of two pounds or over by lunchtime.

Below the ferry the river opens up, sweeping among islands and gravel bars, and Eleazar settled me into serious wading and fishing. The wind was half a gale by this time, but I used the big rod and gave it all it would take. Eleazar was no longer satisfied with the little streamer fly, nor even with a 1x leader. He had seen my dry fly leaders and shifted me down to 3x, which made sense under the bright sun, but his fly changes ranged up and down through the sizes until he had me fishing a No. 1 Silver Doctor on his 3x leader. I protested, with all the Spanish I could muster. "The big fly and the little leader do not go well together," I said, with gestures. "The big one will come and it will break."

He understood but was not at all concerned. "It is okay. You have very good hands. It will not break."

Soon after I hooked a lovely three-pounder in a run of heavy water. I held my breath and let him take everything he would, then steered him into the soft water at the side of the run and handled him like hot coals from a campfire. Eleazar netted him for me and grinned. But he took out my fly box again and considered deeply before selecting a low-water Green Peacock—a lovely little fly on the best of all hooks, but I would still have preferred to fish it with a 1x point.

Wind or no wind, it was a lovely afternoon, a lively time and place to be fishing with a man for whom every

fresh pool was hope, every cast was a thing to watch
and count on. The Green Peacock took a four-pounder,
which was the best fish of the day, from another strong
run. I remember losing a big fish on the Gray Ghost
soon after and killing a nice three-pounder. But the wind
met us more and more strongly as we came nearer the
lake and in the end we knew it was hopeless—there
would be no fishing at the bar that night. So we slid
on down, met the wind full force, and Eufrasio and
Eleazar pounded their way across the head of the lake,
through the trough of the swells, to the beach in front
of the hotel. They were the only boatmen who brought
their boats back from the bar that night. But they were
Zapatas.

Journey to Enco

WE HAD ONE MORE DAY IN PUCON,
but it was a day when business interfered to the exclu-
sion of fishing. I did spend an hour or two on the lake
with Eleazar, taking plankton samples and temperature
readings, checking the bloom of algae blown up by
the previous night's storm and noticing a few dead fish
along the shore line—Chilean pejerreys or silversides and
perca-truchas or white perch for the most part, apparently killed by suffocation. But I had reports to write,
hotels to visit, hotel managers to interview and other
such affairs that Jacko arranged with skill and despatch.

Jacko had long ago taken full charge of me, regulating my comings and goings, my risings and retirings, planning each fishing day to yield maximum experience of the country and the rivers, arranging for boats and boatmen and transportation. He was intensely considerate of me, yet intensely concerned for my honor and prestige, as reflecting that of the airline we represented. All this was on a plane little short of international diplomacy in scope and protocol. I must show a reasonable, but never excessive, generosity in tipping. I must never allow myself to be "cheated" as he called it, or overcharged in any way—and he was a hard bargainer, for he felt that my mere presence in a hotel cast a glow of radiance upon the place, a point of view not always shared by the hotel manager.

He had warned me many times that I must always make a big catch of fish. I protested about that. "But, Jacko, even if I wanted to, I can't always do it. And I don't always want to."

He relented a little. "Perhaps not always. But when there are other boats, always. And you must never let a Chilean fisherman catch more fish than you, or bigger fish."

I didn't know whether to be flattered or shocked by this assumption that I control fate and destiny when I go fishing. But I asked simply, "Why not?"

"Because he would at once go back to Santiago and tell it everywhere. He would make himself very important and say that you are not such a great fisherman, after all."

And over and above all this, there was the matter of the very big fish. There are very big fish in nearly all the rivers of Chile, trout of ten, fifteen, even twenty pounds, and some are caught by fishermen every season. By the time we reached Pucon I had begun to realize that they are nearly all caught during the spring runoff of November and December, or during the fall months of March and early April—almost never in the hot weather of January and February. Yet I was hopeful that somewhere, sooner or later in our travels, a really big trout would stir up from his peaceful summer hiding place and take my wandering fly. Certainly I was determined to keep looking for such a fish and even if I had not been, Jacko would not have let me forget about it for long. At first he had been quite deeply distressed because I would fish only the fly, but when he saw that the fly, day after day, and without fail, took not only more fish, but bigger fish than were taken by the other boats fishing hardware, he became happily reconciled to my use of it. He himself faithfully fished spoons and spinners and plugs, not always from preference but as a valuable check against the effectiveness of my fly, and it was a valuable check, because our boats were seldom more than two or three hundred yards apart during any day, though he usually made sure that his boatman held back and let my boat work first through the pools.

All these things Jacko did out of natural kindness and courtesy and I could not have changed him in them. He was quite unfailingly conscientious in checking any bill he paid for me and the morning we left Pucon, in spite of the hotel's imposing lobby, its multiplicity of bellboys and other servants, and the general dignity of its clientele, was no exception. We were leaving at 7:30 A.M., by a bus which connected with a local train

at Villarica, which in turn, connected with the main-
line expresses for Santiago and Puerto Montt and Loncoche. The bus was pretty full when we loaded our
baggage and Jacko suggested that I hold a seat for him
while he settled the bill. Minutes passed and he did not
appear. The bus driver had started the motor, passengers
began to look at their watches and mutter. I decided to
check on Jacko.

I found him in the center of an admiring group of
bellboys, engaged in fierce argument with the hotel
clerk and another black-coated official who had evidently been summoned to arbitrate. Jacko turned to
me at once. "The fools," he said. "They wish to charge
for a Thermos bottle that was broken in the lunch. It
is an outrage."

"But the bus," I said. "It's waiting. People are getting impatient. Let it go."

Jacko looked as though I had suggested he should
betray his country. "That is impossible. These people
must be shown. The bus will wait. Go out there and
tell him he must wait."

I went back to the bus and stood at the door, with
one foot on the step. "My friend is just coming," I
explained to the driver, who seemed to care little, one
way or the other.

But the passengers cared. They scolded the driver
and told him to go. They looked at their watches and
said they would miss the "combination" at Loncoche,
at Villarica, everywhere. Someone, I suppose, asked the
Spanish equivalent of: "What's it all about, anyway?"
Because someone else said, "It is an argument," and immediately several passengers got up from their seats and

went back into the hotel. They returned quite quickly,
nodding their heads and murmuring approving words.
Three or four minutes later Jacko appeared, climbed
aboard and sat down as though nothing unusual had
happened. There was a murmur of approval, almost
amounting to applause, as the bus started off. "Did you
win?" I asked.

"Of course," he said. "They were quite in the wrong."

As we neared Villarica he leaned forward and slipped
a ten-peso note into the driver's hand. "It is necessary
to stop for a few minutes at the Hotel Yachting," he
told him.

"What are you going to do there?" I asked.

"Find the brass plug of your plankton net that was
lost," he said calmly.

"Don't be silly," I told him. "It isn't important. We're
late already. These good people will go crazy."

"It will be all right," Jacko said. "You will see."

There were some murmurings behind me at the unexpected stop and Jacko's disappearance into the hotel,
but the driver was quite impervious to them and I pre-
tended to be. Jacko appeared in a few minutes with the
missing plug, we drove on to the station, the train was
still there and everyone was safely on board for five or
ten minutes before it moved out.

That was the start of a hard day's travel which took
us through something over a hundred miles to reach a
point about thirty-five miles from where we had started.
The only unusual thing that happened on the next leg
of the trip, from Villarica to Loncoche, was that the
locomotive came uncoupled twice, bringing us to a sharp
stop each time. Of course, we all climbed out to study

the matter and it was quite clear that the whole trouble
was the baggage car, a handsome freak of German make
that had somehow fitted itself in between a British-made
locomotive and coach. The German couplings were so
high that they barely engaged the others at all, and a
slight unevenness in the track was enough to shake them
loose. At the second attempt to tie things together a
brakeman held a fistful of brush against the static cou-
pling and it somehow jammed things securely enough
to hold together through the rest of the trip.

At Loncoche we had a good breakfast, served with
great concern for us, at a tiny but clean hotel near the
railroad. Then we walked to the plaza to find the post
office and mail the letters I had written the previous
day. It was a fairly large post office, but the postmaster
said he had no airmail stamps. I suggested that he sell
me the correct amount in ordinary stamps, but nothing
would persuade him to accept the letters on this basis.
Without airmail stamps, he insisted, they would not go
by airmail, no matter how many other stamps I pasted
on. Jacko did his best to help, but in the end we had
to withdraw, in defeat, the letters still with us.

Our next advance was a short train journey to Lanco,
where a special bus was waiting to take tourists to Panguipulli to catch the lake steamer *Enco*. It was a very
hot day, but we climbed into the bus and waited. Nothing happened. A rumor circulated that the main-line express was two hours late and the bus would not leave
until it arrived. Jacko went out to check and came back
with confirmation of the rumor. The passengers were
indignant or humorous or caustic or merely excited. No
one was resigned, because the bus was already intoler-

ably hot and there seemed to be nowhere else to go. A few people went out into the hot sunshine. A handsome, vigorous woman, Señora Alessandri, daughter-in-law of a greatly respected ex-president of Chile, made excellent fun of the very special nature of our bus—for tourists only, she pointed out, and every passenger must have two ordinary tickets to travel by it, all for the privilege of staying in one place for two hours. She managed to be gracious and funny, tolerant and caustic all in the same phrases and everyone enjoyed her immensely.

After nearly half an hour of waiting I suggested to Jacko that we might reasonably go in search of a beer shop. I was ready to drink beer, quite a lot of it. But before we had taken half a dozen steps from the bus we heard the express coming in. Five minutes later, with aroused but unslaked thirst, we were pounding over the dusty road to Panguipulli.

The *Enco* is a fair-sized lake steamer and the friendly atmosphere of the bus carried aboard her. There was a good cold lunch and plenty of beer. The lake was a gently ruffled blue in the sunlight, with rocky shores and islands and timbered hills—I had to look closely at the hardwood timber of the hills to remind myself that it was not a lake somewhere in British Columbia. A scoutmaster with his group of boy scouts were preparing to cook a lunch on the foredeck. One boy was sent with a bucket and a length of rope to get water from the lake. The *Enco* was making about eight knots and I was pretty certain the idea wouldn't work out too well, but before I could muster a suitable Spanish word the bucket was overside, the pull came on it, the rope jerked out of the boy's hand, and that was that.

The scoutmaster was a commanding, very serious and obviously very practical man. He took an even larger bucket and secured an even larger rope to it. For a moment I had visions of his going overboard, but he tied the rope to the ship's rail and I relaxed a little. He had the right idea, at that. He swung the bucket forward and plopped it into the lake. But he was a little slow in recovering. Only the handle of the bucket came back on the end of the rope. He sent another scout to get water from the *Enco*'s galley.

Jacko came up to me with another bottle of beer. The skipper, he told me, was a wholly admirable man. On this day's trip the ship did not normally put in at the wharf of Chan-Chan, by the outlet of the Enco, which was our destination, but only the port of Choshuenco at the head of the lake. Because we were such distinguished and important passengers, he would happily vary this schedule and land us at Chan-Chan.

I was impressed by this news, but not too surprised because I knew how persuasive, if not commanding, Jacko could be. The *Enco* plowed her way up the lake through the summer afternoon and in the early evening we came to Choshuenco, a cluster of unpainted wooden houses around a small sawmill, with a few planks on flimsy stilts running out into the water. The *Enco* coasted heavily in alongside these and dug her steel nose firmly into the sandy beach. We watched with amusement, even helping a little, as the perspiring passengers struggled off with their baggage and as the freight began to go ashore.

Our pile of baggage, by no means an insignificant item, was in the way and a deckhand began to move some of it ashore. Jacko protested. The deckhand said the ship was not going to Chan-Chan. Jacko said it was. Both appealed to the skipper. The skipper laughed and said of course he was not going to Chan-Chan; that was some other day. Jacko said some rough things to the skipper. The skipper said some rough things back. Soon we were sitting on the beach with our baggage.

The Choshuenco hotel had burned down a year or two previously. The only communication between Choshuenco and Chan-Chan is by winding truck road or by four or five miles of water. Everyone on the beach, and there were many people there, was most kindly disposed toward us, but no one had any very useful suggestion, so Jacko made a trip up to the village while I watched the baggage.

I watched the unloading of the *Enco* and marveled at the cruel awkwardness of unnecessary labor involved. The rickety wharf made less than stable footing for a man and came nowhere near the *Enco*'s deck. It extended for only a few feet up over the soft and yielding sand that made the beach. Nothing was packed for easy handling. A tiny, wizened man of about forty plodded down through the sand, two men loaded a hundred-kilo sack of potatoes on to his back and he staggered away under it. I wondered how many years he would live to work like that and what injuries his body had already suffered.

Jacko came back. He thought he had found a boy with a skiff who would row us to Chan-Chan, and he thought the boy had a friend with another skiff who would take the baggage.

Eventually two small boys with two very leaky skiffs arrived and we divided the baggage and ourselves between them. It was, as a matter of fact, a lovely row down the peaceful evening lake, even though I had to bail all the way to keep my feet dry and the skiff afloat. The Enco's current, drawing down the narrow arm of the lake, helped us a lot and we came almost quickly to the little wharf at Chan-Chan.

We were well ahead of the telegram we had sent from Villarica several days earlier, and I still wonder at the forbearance of Cran and Carmela Kenrick, our host and hostess, whose welcome made the day's travel seem a light thing.

Farm, Forest and River

THE KENRICK FARM IS AN EQUILAT-
eral triangle of about ten thousand acres, having as its
base the Enco River, which flows from Lake Pangui-

pulli to Lake Rinihue, and as its apex the eight-thousand-foot peak of the Volcano Choshuenco.

Ten thousand acres is not reckoned a very large holding in South America, and Chan-Chan rates as a fundo or farm rather than a hacienda or ranch. But its unusual combination of horizontal and vertical distribution makes for considerable diversity of operation; there is hay and pasture land along the flat near the river, some grazing on the first hillsides that rise quickly from the valley, then timber. Much of the timber is good—fine old-growth South American beech in dense stands—and it extends up the hillsides until it peters out on the slopes of the volcano.

Cran Kenrick is a Valparaiso importer and is able to spend only a few months of each summer at Chan-Chan, but the farm is a devotion and a responsibility. He is concerned to restore and build up the pasture lands, but even more concerned to develop the forest land to its full potentiality. In the first two days we were at Chan-Chan we fished a little, in the pools near the house, but Cran found time to ride with us over his land and show us his workings—an opportunity that delighted me, because I always feel that I am fishing in some strange, unreal vacuum unless I know the purpose of the people and the meaning of the country around my rivers.

On the first day we rode downstream through the pastures, seeing the problems of encroaching brush and blackberry vine; Cran said they had not so far yielded to spraying or grubbing and he was wondering if a sizable herd of goats might help. I was impressed by the enormous fences, made by piling heavy, fire-blackened logs into a semblance of riprap. They were the original trees of the valley, long ago burned by settlers who wished to make grazing land out of the forest, and piled into fence lines by ox teams.

Somewhere beyond a little stream called the Pirinel we turned toward the hills and soon came into a deep forest of magnificent hardwood trees. It was a mixed stand of Coihue (a South American beech, Nothofagus dombeyi), Rauli, whose proper name I still do not know, a scented laurel (Laurelia aromatica) and the magnificent Ulmo (Drimys winteri), a type of magnolia growing to full timber size, with handsome glossy leaves and a profusion of ivory white flowers that I learned to look for on forested hillsides all through southern Chile. Most of the trees grew straight and clean for thirty or forty feet from the ground, then forked into double trunks that were still straight and clear of limbs for another fifty feet or so. Many were three feet in breast-high diameter and some were over four feet.

We circled back by a steep trail through the timber until we came to the Pirinel again, crossing just below a fine, bursting white fall, not far from where the stream breaks out of the solid rock of the mountainside. It was a lovely place, dripping with moss and fuschia, surrounded by great trees, cool and moist on the hot afternoon. We climbed a little way up the stream and I checked the temperature of the water—it was only 45° F. As we turned back toward the horses Cran's top hand, who was riding with us, lifted a shrub and showed me a fine olive green tarantula on the underside of it. "She has fed recently," he said. "She is sleepy." It was only then I noticed that even here, in the moist forest, there were no mosquitoes or midges or blackflies, not even Coli-huachos or Tabanos or the little Polcos that sometimes come out along the streams in the late evening.

The next day we went up by the steep truck road behind the farm to see Cran's logging operations. He was logging only dead trees and windfalls, but there are plenty of those because so many of the flat benches of the hillside have been burned for pasture. The logging operation used a combination of oxen, light trucks and oxcarts, though a small tractor arrived while we were at Chan-Chan and I believe Cran had ordered others. Ox teams, working slowly and powerfully, dragged the heavy logs down to the landings and unhitched there. Trucks backed in and were loaded by what we call in the Northwest "parbuckle"—a sling of cable or chain around the log, made fast at one end and hitched to power at the other, so that the pull rolls the log forward into place. Here again the power plant was a yoke of oxen, stepping slowly and accurately over the rough ground and building up a steady strain that used every ounce of their bodies. On the whole, it worked well, though the tremendous weight of the larger logs jarred the trucks cruelly. In the more awkward places, where there were no landings, ox wagons picked up the logs and brought them in.

The operation focused on a temporary sawmill, a simple affair with a head-saw and a small trim-saw, and much heavy hand labor. Oxen brought the logs from the log pound to the carriage of the head-saw, working with wonderful power and precision. Manpower, with ten-foot peavies, took over from there, wrestling the logs into place on the carriage. As the planks came off, there were no live rollers to move them; they passed to the trim-saw on rollers under the hand, and beyond the trim-saw men filed in with thick shoulder pads, to carry the planks away to the piles where they seasoned. I have put in my time on the end of a sorting table in a softwood mill, and curiosity prompted me to heft a few of those planks. The weight of them shocked me.

In that lies the real difficulty in marketing Chile's wonderful hardwood stands. True, there is the other problem of cheap hand labor, which has made the difficult import of costly machinery a doubtful business proposition. But in North America we are used to thinking of logs that float themselves to the market, or at least to the finishing plant. In Chile, in the hardwood forests, logs simply do not float. They have a specific gravity of 1.6 or 1.8, which compares with 0.6 to 0.9 for northern beech and oak, and 0.5 or less for most softwoods. There are no roads or railroads to most of the timber holdings, and the cost of building them is out of proportion to the return. So timber must float to market, or stay in the bush. And timber, in the log, will not float.

The solution is both ingenious and dramatic, and my immediate concern is with dramatics rather than ingenuity. The little haywire mills set up near the scene of logging operations are the first stage of ingenuity. These cut the heavy logs into something that can be handled. The best of it is carried by truck to the lakes, where it can be loaded on barges or perhaps on the decks of steamers like the *Enco*, and economically carried to the railhead. Beyond this, dramatics come into play. The lower grades of lumber cannot be made to pay for their transportation. They will not float themselves to market, so they are piled for a year of seasoning. At the end of this time they will float, though none too well, even then.

At this point the Chilean rivermen go to work. They float the seasoned planks and build them into rafts, some twenty feet square and two or three feet deep. These rafts are built to an ancient pattern, entirely by hand, and are secured by lengths of what looks like heavy (and rusty) telephone wire. I watched the raftmen cinching up on the rafts, using simple levers or their bare hands, and was astonished at the strength and rigidity they could achieve.

Each raft carries three enormous sweeps made of poles about twenty feet long, to which are secured three- or four-foot lengths of plank, quite narrow and roughly shaped into up-curving blades. Two wooden pegs are driven into a block each side of the raft to make oar guides and there are several hardwood blocks, shaped to fit between the pegs and so to raise or lower the leverage of the sweeps. Near one of the oarlocks there is usually planted a strong stick, five or six feet high and with several forks, to carry the clothes of the raftman when he is passing through particularly bad rapids, where the whole raft is often completely buried in white water. Besides the clothes he wears when the water is not too bad, each man has his blanket poncho and a few simple supplies. This, with some spare telephone wire for repairs, is the full equipment for a journey that may last weeks.

Rafts are usually in groups of fifteen or twenty, and there is always a leader who controls and organizes. But the run is made individually, at intervals that seem to be controlled by individual choice or readiness. Sometimes two or three rafts will start out within a few minutes of each other and with the obvious intention of keeping more or less together, sometimes the interval will stretch to several hours and then only a single raft is ready to leave.

I watched many rafts start out as I fished the upper pools of the Enco. Some had come a considerable distance already, down the Fuy River to Lake Panguipulli and so to Chan-Chan, where they paused to be sure of each other's safety and to effect minor repairs. Inevitably, this is serious business, done with care and concentration, and the raftmen impressed me on the whole as very serious men. It is a life work, as I understand it, performed summer season after summer season, and the skill and knowledge are passed from generation to generation. Judging by men who work on water elsewhere, it is a sound bet that not half of them can swim a stroke. Raftmen are drowned every year in Chile, and many more must narrowly escape drowning, so it is not too surprising that they are serious and careful. But they are also proud and confident, and it is a fine sight to see the lonely man moving gracefully to ply his great sweeps, calculating the rapid ahead, guiding the ponderous mass of his raft so that it will come to it at exactly the right point to make safe passage. Whenever I paused to watch a raft ease into the first rapid of the Enco, I felt it to be a moment of strong emotion, a deliberate committal to strain and danger for an urgent purpose.

It was a great satisfaction to be staying within a few yards of a river like the Enco. I was frequently able to go to one or other of the upper pools for an hour or so, either by myself or with a boatman, and I gave the dry fly a good trial. I saw some excellent May-fly hatches and was able to profit by them, catching good numbers of fish up to two and a quarter pounds on floating flies. Some of the surface-feeding fish were taking large green grasshoppers in good numbers and were difficult to move to any floating fly I had, though I took several on wet flies and found their stomachs crammed with grasshoppers. These grasshoppers probably explain the considerable popularity of the Green Highlander salmon fly on the Enco and other Chilean streams.

One day while we were at Chan-Chan, Jacko and I went up to fish the Fuy River, which drains down to Panguipulli from Lakes Pirehueico and Neltume. We transported the boats by truck and oxcart to a point several miles up the river and launched them to perils unknown, because neither we nor our boatmen had seen the river before. It was a bad day, very hot and close, with a thunderstorm that began to play around the summit of the volcano early in the afternoon and which gradually spread over the whole sky. Perhaps because of this we caught very few worthwhile fish; Jacko had one very lovely three-pounder, blue-backed and silver bright, and I found an unrecovered spawner that was an inch or two longer and an ounce or two lighter—the only poorly conditioned rainbow I remember from any of the southern rivers.

But in spite of the slow fishing, there were many things to remember in the day. The river itself was lovely, clear and swift, with several exciting places to run, made the more exciting by being untried. It is a grand river to wade and generally just the right size to cover with a fly rod, so I was wading through most of the day and full of hope that the lovely pools and runs would yield more than the occasional fifteen- or sixteen-inch fish they did. Once a splendid purple-breasted pigeon flew straight across the river to where I was wading under a brushy bank, holding his course until he was within two feet of my face and my eyes looked into his, then swerving sharply so that all his plumage flashed in the sunlight. A little farther down, on a gravelly beach, a big flock of yellowlegs took off, circled and returned—migrants from North America. Below these again, I heard the familiar call of the pileated woodpecker and looked up to see not pileated but magellanic woodpeckers, big, crested birds with the same flight and attitudes as the pileated woodpeckers, the female all black except for a white wing flash and a red patch at the base of the bill, the male with a solid scarlet head and crest.

I remember, too, a thirteen-inch pejerrey that took my fly in a fast run just above the lake and fought like a fish of twice his size, though without jumping; and the wind coming up in uneasy gusts from across the lake as we reached the bar and the great storm breaking fiercely down the slopes of the volcano and the boatmen so obviously concerned by it that we told

them to row on home without waiting to fish the bar
—to their enormous relief. And, last of all the day's
memories, I remember a wild cry, from infinitely far
away, over beyond the storm, and looking up to see
two bandurrias flying a mile above the mountaintops.

The next day, when we had planned to run the Enco
from Chan-Chan to Corte Arena, I was violently attacked by dysentery and could do nothing at all. The
day after I was shaken but better, and we made the
run.

There had been a heavy rainstorm the previous night
and the weather was still cloudy when we started, so
I was hopeful of a good day, even though the river
temperature was 68° F. The Enco is quite a large river
and we covered a lot of very fine-looking water, mostly
by boat, in the morning; but the fishing was very slow
and I think I had only one two-pounder in the boat
when we stopped for lunch just above the mouth of
the Pirinel. I remember losing a larger one which made
a very strong run before throwing the fly, but he undoubtedly was foul-hooked, because there was a scale
firmly fixed to the point of the hook when the fly
came back.

I had felt fairly certain all morning that there would
be a good chance of finding fish where the very cold
water of the Pirinel came into the warm water of the
main river, so I went down there while the boatmen
prepared lunch and Jacko rested. The water of the
little stream was 48° F at the junction and there was
a good rush of it, though tiny in proportion to the
flow of the Enco. I started down with a small Thunder
and Lightning and was into a three-pounder at the first

cast. I beached him safely, cast again and missed a good
fish. The same or another fish in about the same place
took my next cast, ran hard and broke off the gut-
loop eye of my fly. I found another Thunder and
Lightning of the same size in my box, with a metal
eye this time, and tied it on. Within fifteen minutes I
had fished to the end of the influence of the Pirinel
and I had five beautiful rainbows on the beach, the
smallest a three-pounder, the largest a fraction over four
pounds. They were all fat and in perfect shape, and
every one of them had run thirty or forty yards into
the backing behind my fly line.

I had not gone down to the Pirinel with any idea of
doing such execution as this; I had supposed I might
find a good fish or two there, that we would be able
to rest the run through lunch and work it for another
fish or two afterward. So I was a little shamefaced
when I returned to Jacko with my catch—an attitude
that amused him immensely. "It is you who have been
sent out to catch fish, not me," he said. "You should
be pleased for both of us."

As a matter of fact, I was still quite certain that the
mouth of the Pirinel would produce another fish or two
after lunch and so was Jacko—so much so that he refused to fish it at all. So I tried it, with great care and
thoroughness, and could not move a fish. Jacko tried
after that, with flatfish and spoon, and could not move
anything either, but I feel sure that within a day or
two one could have made an equally good catch there.

Fishing was still slow after lunch, but in one long
sweeping reach I picked up two fairly good fish by
telling the boatman to hold harder against the current,

which gave the fly more work. Then I waded down another long, smooth pool just above Corte Arena, and rose a dozen or more fish, all between one and two pounds, by working a fast fly. They came very gently, often two or three times, and I found I could only hook them by holding a loop of line in my hand and releasing it the moment I felt or saw a touch.

Immediately below Corte Arena the river enters a rocky canyon and becomes too fast and wild for boats. We climbed over rocks and fished some of the impressive pools as best we could from the shore. A fast fish took my fly almost at once, right on the reel at the end of a cast, and went away like a torpedo. I am sure he was still running when the fly came back. Farther down, in a slower pool, I took two fish of just under three pounds by working a deep fly, but they were slow and rather lazy, not nearly as active as the fish below the Pirinel. Still farther down, in a pool on a bend, I saw a fish of at least five pounds roll deliberately in good water. He was just beyond reach of any reasonable cast, but I tried him from every angle and feel fairly certain he saw the fly, though he certainly did nothing about it.

It was almost dark by then, but the clouds had cleared away and it was a lovely evening. We walked the three or four miles home by starlight, Jacko and the boatmen singing for much of the way. I was hungry, but Jacko had promised me a good dinner after two days of rigidly controlling my diet. It was a perfect dinner for my need: a small roasted chicken, undoubtedly of a game breed, perfectly browned and nowhere soft; beautifully mashed potatoes, creamy and opaque, with

young carrots and green peas straight from the garden.
The Chilean girl who cooked it admitted that she was
always successful with such things, but insisted she did
not really like to cook.

Journey to Los Lagos

EIGHT OR TEN MILES BELOW CHAN-
Chan the Enco enters Lago Rinihue, a narrow, mountain lake over twenty miles long, which is drained by
the San Pedro, whose waters eventually reach the Pacific Ocean at Valdivia.

Our fairly rigid schedule called for us to fish the
San Pedro next, from the little town of Los Lagos,
which would normally have meant a return by the
steamer *Enco* and the special tourist bus to Lanco, on
the main line, and a train journey from there to Los
Lagos. It seemed that the same thing could be done by
way of Rinihue Lake, rather more easily and quickly
and with the added advantage that we should be traveling new country instead of retracing our steps. There
was a small tug or work boat on Rinihue which could
readily and cheaply be hired to take us down the lake.
A message was sent to her skipper, and as far as we
knew it was satisfactorily arranged that he would be
waiting for us at the little port of Enco, at the head
of Rinihue Lake, between nine and ten o'clock of the
morning we left Chan-Chan.

We left Chan-Chan in good time on a lovely morning and traveled by truck to Puerto Enco, crossing the river by cable ferry just below the entrance of a small stream called, as so many streams are in Chile, Rio Blanco.

The port consisted of a shady wharf, a few tumble-down buildings, a big barn and an extensive lumber-yard. The lake itself was lovely, just beginning to re-spond to a fresh westerly breeze, very blue under the blue sky between untouched slopes of green timber. We found the wharfinger, a good, gentle man, who told us sympathetically that there was no sign of the boat and that he did not really expect it unless it hap-pened to come to pick up a tow of rafts, waiting for it at the mouth of the Enco. With an increasing west wind he thought this unlikely.

We told him our story and he looked hard down the lake. There was no boat in sight, he assured us, and we would see it for at least an hour before it came. I told Jacko to ask if he would rent us a skiff. There was a brand new one in the barn, not quite finished. We launched it and rowed the half-mile or so to the mouth of the Enco with our rods and gear.

Jacko was a little uncertain about the expedition. He was afraid the boat might show up at any moment and turn around again if we weren't there to meet it. But he finally agreed to let me put on my waders and start up the river so long as I promised to be back by noon. He decided he would fish from the boat at the river mouth and keep watch.

I felt fine and free and happy, without boat or boat-man to bother me, though a shade concerned about the time element—an hour or two can go very fast when one is fishing. The rafts we had seen start down from Lake Panguipulli were all safely tied up inside the mouth of the river, twenty or more of them in line along the right bank, with nothing to show they had come through the wild water of the canyon below Corte Arena. The raftmen—balsa-men, I should call them, because everything in Chile that floats, ferry or scow or raft, sometimes even boats, is called balsa, and the proper title of the raftmen is balsa-men—the balsa-men were camped in the bush nearby and I passed the time of day with them as I walked the balsas upstream, climbing over the shocking assortment of rough bits of wire that moored them to the bank. Above the balsas the river was fine, though big to wade and awkward from my side. I didn't care to risk going too far, but started in as soon as I had passed two or three good-looking pools.

Because the day was very bright and because I was near a lake to which I felt sure there would be fry movements, I decided to fish a silver-bodied Iris streamer, instead of the dark, bushy squirreltail flies I had been using in attempt to imitate the apancora. The immediate result was a very fast take from a nice bright two-pound rainbow. A few casts later a considerably larger fish came hard at the fly, missed it twice and would not come again. But in the next pool, which consisted mainly of a very fast deep run almost under my own bank, I hooked a perfect three-and-a-quarter-pounder which I safely netted after a series of awkwardnesses that tangled my rod top in overhanging brush and almost dumped me into the run.

By the time I rejoined Jacko at the mouth I had

three or four good fish, though nothing else as good as the three-pounder. It was a few minutes past noon, the wind had freshened a great deal and Jacko was worried, though he had two or three nice fish in the boat. There was no sign at all of the tug. Jacko had talked with the balsa-men and they had told him they had no set appointment with the skipper—he might pick them up today or he might show up in a week's time, but from the look of the wind it probably wouldn't be today.

Jacko thought we had better row back to the wharf before the wind got too bad. When we arrived there we found a jeep waiting with an invitation to lunch at the guesthouse of the "farm"—a somewhat similar enterprise to Cran's, though much larger and even more concerned with logging operations.

The lunch was excellent, served in a private room with a good measure of ceremony. I asked Jacko why we were so honored.

"It is partly because of Cran Kenrick," he said. "But it is also the hospitality of the country. They can look after twenty people and the place is full now, mainly with a group of students who could not otherwise afford a holiday."

"You mean it's all free?"

Jacko nodded. "It makes good relations for the company in Valdivia. But more than that, they are hopeful the government will build a road along the lake if they can show the place is much used. That is why they are glad we are here."

We walked back to the wharf after lunch, crossing again on the ferry to the great delight of the ferryman, who was deeply interested in our fortunes, as, indeed, the whole valley seemed to be. There was still no news of the boat and the wind was very much stronger, so we settled to read and sleep in the hay of the old barn. The wind whistled through the planks, odd bits of canvas flapped aimlessly, pigs and dogs and chickens passed through, pausing to snort or sniff or cluck near us, but it was pleasant enough there and a welcome refuge from the burning sun. I even puzzled out a theory of temperatures, supported by what I had seen so far in Chile. Obviously the hot summer months of January and February were not ideal for fishing; they seldom are, anywhere. But there were still possibilities. Rivers at 68° F or over were probably altogether too warm for good fishing. Sixty-four degrees, I felt, was probably about the critical point in a stream with a good proportion of brown trout, and 60° F, more or less, was a similar point for rainbows. And even at these temperatures the best fishing would always be off the mouths of cold streams or below heavy runs of broken water, especially in the early morning or late evening. Nothing I saw later in Chile led me to vary these opinions by much.

At six o'clock there was still no sign of the tug, but the farm manager came back in the jeep and invited us up for tea. I was convinced by this time that the ferry would not show and I was more than reconciled to the idea. We could certainly get dinner, and probably beds, at the guesthouse. Between tea and dinner I would start in at the ferry and fish as far down the river as I could. The next day I would get the manager to show us the logging operations.

We went into the guesthouse. We were given cups. We were within seconds of having them filled with tea. Then somebody shouted that the tug was coming, we must get back to the beach right away.

The manager whirled us down to the ferry. The ferryman reported that the tug had gone to the mouth of the river, not to the wharf. The jeep roared off the ferry in four-wheel drive, swung to the left and plowed along a vague bush road until stopped by an old river channel. Jacko and I took off on our feet from there. The tug was slowly pulling away from the river mouth, down the lake. Everyone shouted and waved, but he kept going.

"He has left for Rinihue," Jacko said in despair.

"He isn't towing rafts," I said. "Maybe he's going out to wait for the wind."

"He has gone," Jacko said, and added a few formidable comments on the morality of all boat captains.

"Let's go and talk to the balsa-men," I suggested.

We struggled along over the rocky beach, Jacko pausing every now and then to wave again and shout bravely into the wind. The boat drew slowly away until it seemed to me to pause in shelter behind a point a mile or so down the lake. We came to one of the lesser mouths of the Enco and waded it. Beyond, on the main river, the rafts had been let down almost into the swells at the bar and there was a good deal of activity among the men.

The leader of the balsa-men met us and Jacko questioned him eagerly, then translated his answers for me. "You are right," he said. "They have gone to wait for the wind. If it goes down they will come back for the rafts. If not, he will go back to Rinihue. But the balsa-men will help us shout for him."

They did, but there was no sign of interest or response from the tug. The men were gently sympathetic and very bitter about the captain of the tug. "They say he cares for no one," Jacko reported. "They say he is a pig without manners. They say we can ride on the rafts, but that will be to the start of the San Pedro, not to Rinihue, where we must go." Jacko paused. He was obviously very touched by the sympathy of the balsa-men, as I was. "These are men of the very lowest class," Jacko said. "But see how kind they are."

And good at the job, I thought, watching in fascination the process of assembling the rafts for towing. About fifteen were already in place, securely and closely lashed together. The others came down one at a time in the strong current, one man at the sweeps, another leaping down the line of rafts with a wire in his hands, still others waiting on the end raft to help. It seemed impossible that the awkward, ponderous things could be controlled with any accuracy against the strong current and the heavy swell, but time after time it was done, amid much talk and apparent confusion, with such control and accuracy that each succeeding raft came in behind the others with only inches to be taken up. One man tripped on something and lost his wire, but instantly recovered it; another man cut his hand. But the difficult job was done quickly and perfectly.

As soon as the rafts were all secured the men waved and shouted at the tug again. But there was still no sign of life aboard her. The sun had gone down behind the hills and it was suddenly cold. On one of the rafts there was a big pile of black volcanic sand and some wood. The balsa-men built a fire and we all collected round it, saying bad things about the captain, joking about fish and rafts and rivers and wind. I had given them my fish in the morning. They shared with us bread and onions and red wine.

Much later, when it was quite dark, the wind went down and the tug came in. The captain was a serious, abrupt, but very reasonable young man. He had heard nothing about picking us up, but he would take us.

"And the baggage?" Jacko asked. "It is at the wharf."

"Why is it not here?" the captain asked severely.

"Because," said Jacko meekly, "we did not know you would consent to take us. We were afraid to be stuck with it here on the beach."

This subtle acknowledgment of his power and authority melted the captain completely. He ran over to the wharf and we packed the baggage aboard as quickly as we could in the dark. As we ran back to the rafts he had the forward deck cleared so that we could spread our sleeping bags. I went to sleep watching the fires of the balsa-men and the rise of a great clear moon over the hills. At dawn next morning we left the balsa-men at the entrance to the San Pedro, wishing them well on their journey, saying we hoped to see them along the river. Less than an hour later we found breakfast in the clean little hotel at Rinihue.

Big River

LOS LAGOS IS A PLEASANT, SIMPLE LITtle town, essentially a cattle center and in many ways, I suspect, not unlike similar towns in western North America fifty years ago. Trucks and automobiles were very scarce, horses were everywhere and the railroad, with its daily trains through the center of town, is the most obvious communication link with the rest of the country. It was in Los Lagos, with half the town's population, that I watched the arrival and departure of the Flecha, Chile's streamlined, air-conditioned diesel express that makes the seven hundred and fifty miles from Santiago to Puerto Montt in about fourteen hours. I never traveled by the Flecha—all seats are reserved and they are hard to get in the summer months—but it was a fine thing to see her sliding through the countryside or drawing importantly to a halt at some wayside town.

The Hotel de la France at Los Lagos is as simple and sunny as the town itself, spotlessly clean, very quiet and comfortable. When you want a bath, a maid comes along with a key to turn on the hot water—but the bath is good and hot. When you send out your laundry, you see the familiar garments drying on the line behind the hotel, in a splendor of color and brightness undreamed of until the sun found them there.

The train from Rinihue brought us in too late to fish the first day, but it gave us a chance to see the town. We wandered among the simple stores, buying small things that we needed. I was greatly surprised by the quality of the stores and the variety of goods they carried—the bookstore was especially impressive for such a small town, but I realized later that nearly every town in Chile has a proportionately good bookstore; evidently Chileans make quite a habit of reading.

We wandered into one rather untidy general store because I wanted to buy a red pencil. I saw some unusually handsome huaso sashes hanging in one corner and asked the price of them. The proprietor, a powerfully built, handsome man, with a broad brown face and well-tended mustache, laughed cheerfully. "Those are not for sale. They are mine. I must wear them to ride in the big race at tomorrow's fiesta."

I was a little embarrassed by my mistake—the typical tourist belief that his money can buy anything he sees. "I'm sorry," I said. "But they are very beautiful."

That pleased him no end. "You like that work? You are interested in huaso dress?" I nodded and he spoke to Jacko at length, in what seemed considerable excitement.

Jacko translated for me. "He says he wants to take you to see the girl making the huaso sashes and ponchos—his sister-in-law, I think. He says to see how the colors match in his sash and poncho and the band for his sombrero. He will show us the saddle and bridle and stirrups and spurs he will use."

There was, of course, no refusing such an invitation. Our friend closed his store immediately and we set off at a great pace down a side street, to a little corner shop with a hand loom in the window and a blue and white silk dress poncho partly finished, still on the loom.

The back of the shop was hung with sashes and ponchos in every combination of colors.

As we filed in through the door a small, quick, black-
eyed girl came into the store from a back room. We
were introduced, our mission was explained and without the slightest hesitation she began to show us her
work. First she went to the loom and swiftly ran a
few more heavy threads of brilliant silk into the blue
and white poncho. From the loom she flew like a bright
bird to the walls, took down half a dozen sashes and
began instantly to model them, switching them about
herself in many graceful ways, moving her body so that
the sunlight caught the colors and brought them alive,
laughing and talking without pause. She wore a white
and gold sash for us, a plain green one, another that
was green and black and gold, many others with reds
and greens and blues, orange, white or black in them
—any color that was strong and bold and clear.

Our friend's bridle and reins were there, decorated
with woven bands that matched the red and green and
blue of his sash. Only the headstrap was different—it
was red, white and blue. He pointed to it.

"What color is that?" he asked, very seriously.

They were all three quite silent, the horseman, the
girl and Jacko, waiting intently for my answer. Fortunately, I knew it could only be one thing. "For
Chile," I said.

They laughed and cheered and slapped me on the
back. Then the girl asked, "And for Canada?"

I was ashamed to admit I did not know. "Red and
gold and green," I said.

"Why is that?" the girl asked.

"For the leaves of the trees," I told her.

"It is very beautiful," she said.

From there we went to the farrier's and saw the heavily roweled spurs and the handsomely carved wooden stirrups, polished and glowing like ancient ivory. Then to the saddler's, to admire the full-fleeced sheepskin and magnificent leather, carefully inlaid with little patches of woven blue silk that matched the sash and poncho.

"It must cost him a small fortune," I said to Jacko.

"For a poor man it is very much. The saddle alone is worth fifteen thousand pesos. Tomorrow, in the race, he may win ten thousand pesos."

We all went into a wineshop and drank to Chile, to Canada and to our friend's success next day.

Later, in the bar of the hotel before dinner, we boasted to the hotel proprietor of our friend and his equipment. The proprietor was a very serious, almost a gloomy man, but he laughed without restraint at Jacko's admiring description, then did some explaining.

"He says he knows him very well," Jacko told me. "He is the town no-good. He owes everybody money and will never pay. But he will win the race tomorrow. He has a very good horse."

We fished the San Pedro next day from Malihue suspension bridge to Los Lagos, a run of thirty kilometers, which is very much too long for one day's fishing. One is forced to hurry over much good water and there is never time to stop to wade and work thoroughly through a good pool. The fault was mine, of course, because I was trying to see too much in too little time. But long runs are a common fishing fault in Chile, and nearly all the traditional boat runs on the big rivers are much longer than they should be.

The San Pedro is a big river, and it is unquestionably a big fish river—a twenty-pound brown trout was caught there in March 1937 and fish between ten and twenty pounds have been relatively common; Cran Kenrick showed me several he had caught in the river and had had mounted. It is also a very beautiful river, generally swift flowing, often broken by runs and rapids and gravel bars, passing through rolling agricultural country with magnificent trees and little settlement. But it has long smooth stretches of relatively unbroken current, too deep for wading, far too wide to cast into, and these can seem very dull to an impatient fisherman, which I am, even though they certainly hold big fish.

I remember of that first day some fine strong water, broken and complicated by many islands, up near Malihue. The boatman worked it well for me in the bright sun and gave me a chance to wade wherever he could, but I think the biggest fish I caught there was under two pounds. I remember the powerful upstream wind, which blew all day long, and some fine deep pools between high tree-clad banks, from one of which I took a brown trout of nearly five pounds. Most clearly of all I remember seeing my first Chilean kingfisher, almost identical with our own northern belted kingfisher, possibly a little larger, but with a solid scarlet breast. He called and flew and fished exactly as our bird does, and I found great pleasure in him.

At lunchtime we met a pleasant Belgian and his wife, who had to leave Los Lagos that night and were fishing through the same stretch in half a day. They knew nothing of fishing, they told us, but it seemed a pleasant sport. They had caught a magnificent brown trout, deep-bodied and golden, of just over five pounds on a Terrible—a slotted silver devon minnow with three sets of treble hooks, bought in Los Lagos the previous day. "Did I think it a good type of lure?" they asked anxiously. Of necessity, I thought it very good indeed. They were extremely civilized people, as full of wonder at the loveliness of Chile as I was, and the four of us lunched happily together, talking French and Spanish and English. I was sorry when they had to hurry on to catch their train at Los Lagos.

After lunch the river grew wider and the country around it flatter. Dreaming along in the boat, I calculated that we had passed over one good long day's fishing between Malihue and the ferry at Melefquen. Just below the big rocks I thought there was half a day's casting in one pool that the boat had to leave unworked, because a boat cannot work it. But I was hopeful of a tributary Cran had described to me, the Quinchilka, which enters on the left bank. When we came to it we found the hot summer weather had left only a trickle of water, flowing at a little over 70° F. I fished the mouth, and the main river below the mouth, but I cannot remember that there was anything there.

By that time it was getting late and there was still a long way to go. Most of the rest of the way was a row home, and it was almost dark when we reached Los Lagos. I had some fish in the boat at the end of the day, and I had enjoyed many things, but it hardly seemed a day of fishing.

We made a considerably shorter run the next day,

from Los Lagos to Purey. First of all we searched the quiet water near the town, looking for a big fish near the outlet from the slaughterhouse. I was quite hopeful of that and gave it a good try, but I caught only brown trout of about two pounds each.

Then we came to some lovely water, broken by low islands, sparkling brightly over gravel bars, running hard under shady banks. I got out on to my feet at once and began to fish a short quick little pool behind an island. It carried perhaps only a tenth of the water of the river, but it had deep, broken places in it and a splendid run entering at the head. I took two fish from it, good clean rainbows, each shading two pounds. There were more good runs below, still behind the island, but I could find only small fish of twelve or fourteen inches in them, so I turned back to the main channel.

It broke over a gravel bar, very fast and clear and bright in the strong sunlight, a long, tearing run, too strong for fish to hold in but with a slackening along the edge that gradually spread through the pool. Two more fish, both over two pounds, took my squirreltail quite promptly and the boatman netted them for me. Then, about one-third of the way down the pool, I struck into a solid fish that turned into the current and tore off fifty yards of backing without a sign of stopping. At the end of that he jumped and I could plainly see the blue back and silver belly of perfect condition. But he was disappointingly small; a four-pounder, I thought. He fought all the way to the net, running two or three more times well into the backing and jumping superbly against the broken, lively water. I netted him well down the pool, in the slack water of the eddy, and weighed him at once: exactly three and a half pounds.

It looked like a fine start to a good day and the flatness of the country ahead made me hope that the river would continue to spread and break over gravel bars. We found one more good run, which Jacko fished conscientiously without finding anything. Then we were embarked upon enormous slow flat reach that seemed to go on and on forever. It lasted till lunchtime and carried on beyond where we stopped for as far as I could see, to a broad bend by a high cut-bank. It was good water in its way and we took from it several brown trout that weighed between two and three pounds. The elusive monster might have been anywhere in it, but I felt that if he had been he would have been only a statistic—not, like the three-pounder below the gravel bar, a fish to remember.

Lunch was a pleasant interlude, on a grassy slope below a grain field, under good shade trees. The hard downstream wind did not bother us there, but rushed over us, up in the treetops.

Jacko said, "You don't like the big rivers so well as the smaller ones. Why is that?"

"I don't like them when they are dull and flat like this," I said. "And you know I don't like them when we have to go too far in a day. That's all right for a boat ride, but not for fishing."

"You will like Rio Bueno. It is here or in Rio Bueno you will catch the big fish."

"I'm not sure I care too much about big fish," I said. "Three- or four-pound fish in the right place are just as good. We ought to enjoy them instead of worrying about that monster."

Jacko was a little shocked. "But it is most important for you to catch one. The airline would want you to catch one. You are a famous fisherman. It will look very bad if you do not."

I laughed. It was fine to be called a famous fisherman. "Don't pay too much attention to me," I said. "Of course, I want a big fish and I'll keep on looking hard for one. But I don't think we ought to let it interfere with enjoying the fish we do catch. We've had wonderful trout fishing by most standards every day we've been out."

"You won't try the flatfish or a spoon?"

"Maybe. When you catch bigger fish with them than I do with the fly."

"But you are a much better fisherman. You would be able to catch a big fish if you used such things."

"I don't think so," I said, sincerely enough. "If I'm going to get one I'll get him on the fly just as well as anything else."

"You think you will get one?"

I considered that carefully. "Sooner or later. I think so. Perhaps even this afternoon. But the temperature of the water is against it. Big fish are lazy in warm water. Remember, no one we have seen so far has caught bigger fish than us, except the Belgian yesterday, and his was only a few ounces bigger."

Jacko seemed satisfied and I lay back to enjoy the peace of the bad hour. The boatmen were asleep somewhere in the grain field above us, wrapped in their ponchos. Some wise spirit had urged me to order two full bottles of wine for Jacko and myself in that day's lunch and I enjoyed it to the full. Lying back I could feel its flush on my cheeks, its gentle ease in my body. The boatmen would sleep for at least an hour, longer if we let them. There was a little run of water below the boats that I had promised myself to fish just before they were ready to go, but nothing else was on my conscience, not even Jacko's big fish.

I found myself hoping that I should always remember how fully and deeply I had loved Chile. Even this day, by that big, flat, dull pool of the San Pedro, with the wretched boats (and they were wretched, the worst I saw in Chile) waiting for us at the water's edge, with the fierce downstream wind waiting to tear at us the moment we left the hollow of shelter we were in, even this day was a time of happiness and well-being. I was lying under a little roble tree, looking up at the sky through its leaves. Near it were two or three native acacias, and beyond these an ulmo tree in full ivory blossom. From the roble and the acacias little scarlet vine-flowers hung in touching brilliance, seeming too frail for the wind of that place. Little harmless white clouds were all over the sky, but not one had seriousness of purpose enough to touch the sun. I could turn my head and look out across the river at summer-browned fields and scrub timber and lines of poplars marching the boundaries. Queltegues called without ceasing, distant, harsh, yet excitingly musical. Someone, long ago, had stopped at the little roble tree to nail up a board fence that once extended to the edge of the summer river. A truck thundered in all its rare glory along some faraway road. A horseman, crossing the field

on the far bank, stirred a dust cloud that followed him
on the wind.

Jacko stirred beside me and said it was time to go
and wake the boatmen or they would happily sleep
until the sun went down and left them cold. I picked
up my rod and went to the smooth, gliding run I had
promised myself to fish.

There was more smooth, dull water through the afternoon, but I fished conscientiously, searching for the big
fish. I even put a queer little plug called a "Hot-shot"
on one of my fly rods and let it hang out behind the
boat. One I had given Jacko at the Trancura bar had
proved astonishingly effective in catching perca-truchas,
the so-called Chilean native trout which is not a trout
at all but a white perch and which I suspect may not
be a native either but some early introduction of the
Spanish settlers. It caught me a long thin brown trout
that should have weighed four pounds and did weigh
less than three; then it caught so many perca-truchas
that I took it in because it was a nuisance. It was an ex-
traordinarily selective lure for these fish, as we proved
again in a later trial.

Even on the dullest and flattest stretch of water there
is a good deal a fly fisherman can do to help his boatman, and I did it all. I kept up a steady beat of the rod
top, watching the line closely all the time for the least
sign of a touch on the fly. I lifted and cast accurately
into places where a swirl suggested some submerged
obstruction or where the set of the current seemed to
make a good feeding lie. I hung my fly deep and slow,
tried it fast and shallow, held it over with the rod against
banks which the boat could not reach. And we caught

trout, mostly brown trout of well over two pounds, but never a monster among them.

Toward evening we came to more interesting water. It was still boat water, but water with force and life to it, and breaks and runs where one could at least expect to find a fish. Something slow and solid did hold my fly for a moment, even started to run out line in the slow solid way of a heavy brown trout; then the fly was free again. Twenty yards downstream I killed a well-conditioned brown trout several shades paler in color than those we had been catching.

We passed a bank where a powerful current had cut in heavily. Someone had put up a line of great log tripods, bound with wire and filled with rocks, to protect the bank, but the water had cut behind them and attacked again, so that the tripods were left in the stream. As the boatman worked slowly past them, I laid my fly against every one, above it, below it, along the side, always hoping that some big fish would be using its shelter. Nothing moved to the fly.

Then, very suddenly, there were gravel bars and little islands and dancing water again. I went out into it at once and hooked a lovely rainbow very quickly. Farther on, still wading, I found the best brown trout of the day, a pale three-pounder, beautifully marked, which jumped three or four times and ran hard in the strong current. Below me there were gravel bars and more good water for as far as I could see, and where the river turned a lovely, leaping white rapid.

Jacko came past in his boat and I saw him pointing toward the left bank. "The truck," he said. "This is where we stop. It is eight o'clock."

I told my boatman to go on, I would wade down. I found another two-pound rainbow on the way and, just to show him I meant no harm, let him go.

As we loaded the boats I saw a bare-legged native fisherman wade in at the head of the big rapid below us, with his twenty-foot bamboo pole and a crayfish on a big hook. Beyond him I could see half a mile of good, broken water. I envied him. At least he knew where to start in and he had the best hour of the day ahead of him. I hope he caught a monster—or at least a three-pound rainbow.

Lago Maihue and the Calcurrupe

I FIRST HEARD OF LLIFEN AND LAGO Maihue and the Calcurrupe River from my friend Eddie de Rothschild when we were fishing a swollen British Columbia stream in May. When he heard I was going to Chile, Eddie wrote to urge me again not to miss the place. He was quite right. Though my stay there was far too short, I think Llifen may well be the best fishing center in Chile.

Jacko had never been there and was a little dubious about it, though not about the fishing. "It will be very primitive, quite cut off from civilization at the head of Lago Ranco," he said. "Probably the food will be very bad." With that he stocked up on candy bars, biscuits, canned fruit and Nescafé in Los Lagos.

The journey was longer than most we made between stops, but it went smoothly and comfortably through lovely country. A main-line train took us sixty or seventy kilometers to La Union, where we changed to a branch line for the port of Lago Ranco, where the lake steamer started her run to the head of the lake. The last few miles of the train journey took us down a long, twisting incline, with perpetually changing views of the lake, all quite lovely.

Herr Ziegler, the founder of Llifen, was aboard the lake steamer. He is a big, strong-voiced, strong-willed German, a former merchant seaman who had been interned in Australia during the first war. Upon his release—or escape, as he told me the story, with suitable and bloody details—he came to Chile and built the first steamboat to ply the waters of Lago Ranco, which is a sheet of water some twenty miles square, with many inlets and tributary valleys and thirteen considerable islands. His venture prospered, he bought the farm of Llifen and built the small hotel which his daughter and son-in-law now own and run.

Herr Ziegler was friendly, welcoming and confident, an expansive host to the glories of his country, his rivers, his lakes. He was sure we should have good fishing—it would be better, of course, in December or March, but the rainbows of Lago Maihue and the Calcurrupe were always there. They were big—up to almost five kilos. And they fought as no other fish fight; he preferred them in the lake—"in the river they fight too hard."

He was not selling us, only telling us glories he believed in. And he had little need to sell us. It was a lovely evening, settling to calm after a windy day. The little lake steamer plowed her way efficiently along, the mountains at the head of the lake grew larger, more grandly rugged as we drew nearer, even though the sun had gone far down and only the night sky backed them. When we docked in the dusk at the little wharf I had just a single worry left—I was very hungry and after Jacko's predictions I wondered what sort of dinner would be waiting.

We walked a hundred or two hundred yards along a dusty road from the wharf, Herr Ziegler bade us good night at the door of his house and we went on to the hotel. Our hostess, a lovely blond girl, greeted us warmly and showed us to attractive rooms, full of flowers, with a tender arrangement of lampshades and counterpanes and curtains in which I was sure Herr Ziegler had had no part. There was a private bathroom between our rooms. The only sign of the primitive, as I pointed out to Jacko, was in the thinness of the walls and floors, through which every sound of the hotel came plainly to us. But Jacko was even more impressed than I was. "It is obvious they have made a big difference," he said. "About dinner, we shall see."

Half an hour later we were in the big, bright dining room. It was full of young people, younger people than I had seen in any hotel in Chile. The food was abundant and good, the wines were excellent. Afterward, the bar was a friendly, hospitable place, and the barman knew exactly how to please everyone.

Llifen offers so many alternatives of good fishing that it is hard to choose between them. At least five streams flowing into Lago Ranco are within reach—Calcurrupe, Nilahue, Rininahue, Cahuenahue and Quiman—as well as Lago Maihue and the streams that flow into it: Hueinahue, Carran, Rio Blanco and Quinileifu. I knew I wanted to see Lago Maihue and run the Calcurrupe, so that was an obvious first day's choice. For the second day I suggested to Jacko we should pick the stream that seemed to offer the best chance of a really big fish. This narrowed the choice to the Rininahue, where a fish of thirteen and a half pounds had been caught the previous season, and the Hueinahue, which had produced a fish of 9.9 pounds almost as recently. I chose the Hueinahue, because it was farther back in the mountains and likely to be colder, though I suspected that the big fish of either stream must have made their growth in the lake below.

To run the Calcurrupe we drove some ten or fifteen miles by truck over fair gravel roads to the little sawmill at the foot of Lago Maihue. The lake lies well back among the high hills, a narrow sheet of lovely water, and I was a little doubtful about its fishing possibilities until I saw the shallows and reed beds at the outlet of the Calcurrupe. One boat had arrived before us and was fishing already, with two anglers sitting side by side and trailing lines from the stern. I saw them with fish almost at once. Jacko put out a flatfish and began to troll. He also had a fish rather quickly, while I was still taking temperature readings and making a plankton sample. It was a good bright rainbow of about two and a half pounds.

I was a little doubtful about how to start in on a strange lake where I had no idea what manner of creature the fish would be feeding on. But I supposed the apancora would be there, as they were everywhere else, so I put up a small squirreltail and told my boatman to row slowly along within casting distance of the reed beds. I rose a fish fairly quickly, but he came short to the fly and would not come again. I kept pitching the fly in, close against the reeds and rose two or three more fish, all good ones of two or three pounds, but not one was securely hooked. Jacko passed near me and was horrified when I told him I had nothing.

"But I have five, all good ones, like this," he said, holding up a two-and-a-half-pounder, "and the other boat has more. You must do something or it will be very bad. We must start down the river very soon."

I did something. I changed my fly. I think I changed it to a Norton, but I'm not sure. It rose two more good fish and one of them was almost in the net when the fly came away. My boatman had taken me well down into the river current, though I could still reach the reeds and I was putting the fly right into them, often between the stems, with a control and accuracy that pleased me considerably. Jacko's boat came down again with the other boat following.

"They have stopped taking," he said. "So we are going down to the lunch place. You had better come too."

"Sure," I said. "I'll be right along."

"How many have you caught?"

"None," I said.

"Impossible," Jacko said, and I knew he felt that all honor was forever lost—for me, for him and for the airline.

There wasn't much to say, so I pitched the fly at the edge of the reeds again. It landed beautifully, not an inch from the nearest stem, and immediately came right back out again in the mouth of a wonderful trout, at least a six-pounder. Before I could tighten on him he was back in the water and out again, ten feet nearer the boat. Altogether I think he jumped twelve times, straight out each time, head up, tail down, two or three feet clear of the water, each time at some different, altogether unexpected place, but never more than fifty feet from the boat. I handlined frantically, but can't remember that I ever did tighten on him. Around the seventh or eighth jump he threw the hook. Even at the moment I couldn't regret it properly—no other fish I have ever hooked has put on quite such a breathtaking performance, and it was obvious from the first that he was lightly hooked. But I couldn't tell Jacko that. "Don't worry," I said with reasonable confidence. "I'll pick up two or three before I start down."

I changed my fly again, but I was still thinking in terms of my limited Chilean experience and all the new fly achieved was three more missed rises—I don't think one of the fish was hooked, even for a moment.

I felt sorry for my boatman—a silent boy of eighteen or twenty named Aquilera—as we started down the river. Yet he had been able to laugh with me over the six-pounder that threw the hook, laughter that was a little awed by the size of the fish, but of the right kind. He had just the right smile of half-humorous commiseration, too, as I swore ruefully, and with progressive emphasis, over each fish I missed. I felt he wasn't too discouraged about it all, but I was sorry to have inflicted such a morning upon him.

Lunch was a wonderful interval. We found the others stopped at a pleasant sandy beach on a bend of the river. The big fire was already going. A table of heavy driftwood planks had been set up between log seats under the shade of some trees; the wine bottles, red Tocornal, were already set out on it, with a long loaf of bread, cheese, butter, plates, cutlery and drinking cups. The two men from the other boat were George Delano and Henry Ross, both Chileans, from Valparaiso, and members of the Club Pesca y Caza of Valparaiso, by far the most active rod and gun club in Chile.

They had a lovely catch of fish, seven two-pounders between them which, with Jacko's five, made a noble display. We took a few pictures while the boatmen were cooking lunch and I checked a random sample of the fish. Without exception, they had been feeding on sedge larvae with bright green cases, built from reed stems. I began to understand why my flies had been getting short rises, though I have to admit that one or two of Henry's fish had been taken on a fly just as unlike the green sedge as my own. The fish were astonishingly level in size, varying only a few ounces from the average of two and a half pounds, and all about eighteen inches long. I supposed at the time that they were all more or less in the same age group, but found later they varied from three- to five-year-olds.

Henry and George were wonderfully good company. Henry was a short, dark quick man of about thirty, who had studied at Oxford and spoke beautiful English; George had iron-gray hair and a dry, easy way of talking that was a perfect complement to Henry's enthusiasm. From the moment we sat down together it was as though we had been friends for years and shared a hundred fishing lunches. We traded talk of fishing in Canada and fishing in Chile, and after a while the Tocornal moved us on to talk of other things, theater and books and music, Europe, New York, Argentina, Montreal, Oxford, Santiago, drinking toasts to most of them, until George settled down on the sand between the log and the table and said it was time to go to sleep. Henry and Jacko agreed and I was about to go along with the idea, when Jacko pointed out that Aquilera was waiting for me, ready to go. "He wants to show you some special places," Jacko said. "For the dry fly and wet. He has never seen the dry fly."

I had been told that Aquilera was a keen fisherman, that he often went to the river by himself when there were no tourists to guide and that he fished both wet fly and apancora with considerable effect. The thought of being shown the special places of boyhood discovery was too much for me and I gave up the idea of sleep, because Jacko was telling me, as plainly as his unfailing courtesy would let him: "Get on out there and catch some fish."

There was some fairly smooth water just below our lunch place, nicely broken by shallow bars and runs, and I fished a dry fly over it quite carefully. The fish responded well, but they were all small, not over a pound and a quarter. I tried a wet fly and it was just the same. Aquilera shook his head. "This place is no good today. There are better places farther down."

I had checked the water temperature at 64° F at 9:00 A.M., so I was fairly sure that if we were to catch big fish in the river it would be in heavy, broken water. Evidently Aquilera had the same idea. We ran far downstream without stopping, to a splendid, straight, whitewater run that scarcely slowed enough to make anything that could be called a pool. I waded in and fished down it, finding two good rainbows of just under three pounds each. As I was netting the second one Jacko came along and fished a deep fast pool at a bend below the run. Aquilera and I went down and joined him, and while we were talking I threw out a fly and hooked another fish, a little smaller than the two in the boat. Jacko was pleased.

"Where are Henry and George?" I asked.

"They're coming," he said. "Your boatman wants you to go on to another place. This is not the best. He didn't think you would get such good fish here."

So we ran on until Aquilera stopped at the head of a little rocky island between two chutes of roaring white water that were almost falls. He signaled me to fish the upper run, between the island and the right bank. It was a narrow, awkward place, spreading to a deep back eddy on my side, but I rose a good fish at once and missed him. Then another fish took solidly and I netted him safely, a three-pounder. I fished out the pool without another touch, but took a two-and-a-half-pounder from alongside a sunken log in the little pool immediately below.

As I turned back to the big run on the outside of the island Henry and George rode through it, cheering and waving, with Jacko closely behind. They kept on going and disappeared from sight around a bend.

The first fish I hooked, right at the edge of the white water of the big run, was the strongest fish I hooked in Chile. He ran at once, across the fast water and about forty yards down, then began to work back up in the eddy on the far side. I moved down a little until I was below him, then began to ease him gently across. To my surprise he came, very nicely, and I began to think he was under control. Then he chose to run. There was no question of stopping him or turning him. He just ran. When he had my fly line and about seventy-five yards of backing out, I began to run too. When I caught up to him he was holding nicely, in quite shallow water over a little bar where the channel I was fishing rejoined the main river. It was a good position. The water below me was not too bad and I could still follow if I had to. Aquilera was there to help with the net. I didn't think the fish had a chance. Then the leader broke at the fly.

I was using a 9/5 nylon leader and there was no great strain on the fish—not nearly as much as there had been several times earlier in the affair. I suppose the material was fatigued at the knot and I should have known enough to retie my fly before chancing such strong water. I haven't the least idea how big the fish was, but from what happened later I feel fairly confident he was not under five pounds.

I went back to the white water, put on another leader and quickly caught two beautiful fish, one of three and three-quarter pounds and one just over four, both of which made long downstream runs, though not so long as the first fish. Then I hooked a still larger fish which seemed to be absolutely uncontrollable. He ran well down and across, then back, jumping several times. I managed to bring him over to my side, but he ran again and after that chose to fight in the heaviest water, letting me gain on him occasionally, but always taking line again. I was well below him and finally he seemed to tire. I brought him toward me, against the flow of the deep eddy on my side, but he held deep in spite of all my lifting. Then, somewhere straight out from where I was standing, everything stopped.

I looked at Aquilera and saw he was on tiptoe, trying to stare down into the deep water. "Snagged," I said, and Aquilera nodded sadly.

I began to wade out, rather cautiously because the gravel sloped steeply, still holding a strain on the line. When I was almost at the top of my waders the bottom leveled off and I felt more hopeful. I edged forward, shading my eyes to try and see down to the bottom. Then I could see a long dark log, eight or ten inches through. Wedged under it, flat on his side, shining up at me, was my fish. There was only one thing to do. I waded forward two more steps, filling my waders, took careful aim and kicked the poor fish in the nose. He was so tightly wedged that the first kick didn't move him. I kicked again, two or three times. He came free and he was beat—four and three-quarter pounds hooked in the pectoral fin.

That seemed to be all we needed, Aquilera and I. It is a longish run down to the lake from those pools, and we fished a little on the way down, but mostly we just rowed happily along.

Back at the hotel Jacko and Henry and George were waiting on the veranda as Aquilera dumped our catch in the light. I don't think I have ever seen Jacko happier. He pulled out the two four-pounders and held them up for everyone to see.

"Beautiful," he said. "Beautiful. I knew you would find them."

"Aquilera found them," I said. "He did better than that, too. But do I get a drink before I change?"

Henry slapped me on the shoulder. "We were waiting for you," he said. "There's one already mixed."

Abortive Expedition

WE STARTED OUT EARLY NEXT MORNing for Lago Maihue. Everything, Jacko said, was arranged. There was a tug on the lake in which Herr Ziegler owned half share. It was coming down the lake with a tow and would be in when we arrived or soon after. We had a letter from Herr Ziegler to the captain of the tug telling him to place himself, his boat and his crew at our disposal for the whole day. He would take us, with our boats and boatmen, to the mouth of the Hueinahue, halfway up along the north shore of the lake, and would wait there for us until we were tired of fishing and ready to go home.

Having been familiar with logging operations and towboats for a good half of my life, I was considerably impressed. "It is quite natural," Jacko told me. "Herr Ziegler owns half the operation and half the boat. He is also interested in the hotel and the tourists. There is money to be made from both. When it is needed for tourists, the lumbering can wait a little. It is a very sensible arrangement."

I reflected that things of this sort are handled more rationally and calmly in Chile than elsewhere, and hoped for the best.

When we arrived at the lake there was no tug in sight, but that was reasonable enough; Ziegler had said it might be late. I was glad, because I had some theories about Maihue Lake trout and hoped to retrieve my failures of the previous morning—perhaps even to try another conclusion with the jumping six-pounder.

Conditions were not of the best; the lake was glass still under a brilliant sun. The magnificent Great Grebes, which I had first seen at Villarica Lake, were swimming serenely, leaving smooth wakes behind them on the surface of the lake, arching their long red-brown necks and raising their jet-black crests. The little water hens that skittered and played near the reeds sent out ripples that never seemed to die. I put up one of the big emerald green dragon nymph imitations that Bill Nation used to tie for the Kamloops trout lakes in British Columbia, and threw it at the edge of the reeds. It flopped right in there and before I could retrieve it at all it was firmly taken by a fish of two and three-quarter pounds. I congratulated myself on my skill and knowledge and the vast experience that let me solve

these things so easily, and kept on fishing. The next
fish that rose to the big fly missed it completely, came
again on a second cast and missed again. That, I felt,
could happen to the best of flies and the best of fishermen.

I kept casting at the reeds for fifteen or twenty minutes more without result, then a good fish followed the
retrieve and swirled twice without touching the fly.
Two or three casts later another fish came up, plucked
at the fly and was not hooked.

That reduced me to a proper state of humility. Nation's big nymph was tied on a No. 1 hook. I cut back
to a similar dressing on a No. 4 hook and killed the
next two fish I rose. Then we saw the tug coming
down the lake with its tow. Jacko said we had better
move in toward the sawmill and wait for it. There was
plenty of time, so I fished all the way over and missed
two more good fish on the new fly. As we came to
the sawmill I took it off and put on a No. 6 green
sedge, the fly I should have put on in the first place.
It was rather smaller than the larvae the fish were
feeding on and not so bright in color, but under those
midmorning conditions of bright sun and still water it
would have been taken with more confidence. I decided
I would test the idea at the mouth of the Hueinahue,
where George and Henry had told me there were shallows and reed beds much like those at the outlet of the
lake.

The captain of the tugboat took some time getting
rid of his tow in a corner of the bay, but eventually
he came over to the wharf where we were waiting.
The tug was a sizable craft, forty or fifty feet long

and steam-powered. The captain was a clean-shaven, tidy-looking man of about thirty-five. He didn't seem especially pleased to see us; in fact, he was at first obviously evasive, then short, but Jacko finally handed him Herr Ziegler's letter and I felt that all would be well. He read it quickly and handed it back. "It is impossible," he said. "I have no time to be running tourists around."

Jacko protested. We were no ordinary tourists. We were making a survey of the fishing. It was a matter of grave economic importance. The captain didn't care about that. He had his work to do and he had no time.

Jacko protested again, with all the eloquence at his command and I began to feel sorry for the captain. Undoubtedly, he did have his work to do; running tourists around would naturally seem a rather pointless occupation. Then he made a mistake.

"It would be impossible anyway," he said. "I have no wood."

"You can get some."

"It would take all day. And anyway, I do not take orders from the hotel or from Herr Ziegler."

"Herr Ziegler has a half interest in the boat," Jacko said. "It is natural he should give orders."

"It is not the important half. I do not take orders from it."

The argument went on and on, and I lost interest in it. It seemed to me that a trip up and down the lake with a character as surly as this one would be a wasted day in any case.

"Jacko," I said. "Tell him if it takes more than half an hour to load enough wood to run that thing of his up and down the lake, he's the lousiest skipper I ever heard of. And tell him I wouldn't go aboard that awkward-looking, unstable tub of his if he went down on his knees and begged me to."

"What shall we do then?"

"Run the Calcurrupe again," I said. "Go ahead, tell him."

Jacko told him, and I signaled my boatman to pull away. When Jacko caught up with me he said, "I told him all you said. And I told him, too, that I will go straight back to the hotel and make a very big scene. He will be fired. You will see."

"You'll have to tell them," I agreed. "In case someone else gets stuck the same way. But you won't have to say much. They'll be more upset than we are."

"I shall make a scene," Jacko insisted. "You don't understand how these things are. This is a man of the artisan class, he has had a little training and knows nothing, but he has to show his authority. They are stupid people, not true Chileans at all. They have no courtesy."

"He's a tugboat skipper," I said. "They're the same everywhere. They don't take orders from anyone if they can help it. Look at the guy on Rinihue and the skipper of the *Enco*."

"You mean it would be the same in your country?"

I thought of all the obstinate, autocratic, fanatically independent tugboat skippers I had known in the logging camps of British Columbia; kind-hearted men, willing to do anything in the world to help out a fisherman, woodsman, even an ordinary traveler, so long as it came to them as their own idea, of their own bounty,

not as an order with the weight of an office desk behind it. "Sure," I said.

Jacko shook his head in disillusionment. "Just the
same, I shall make a scene. A very important scene.
You will see."

I meant to enjoy what was left of the day with
Aquilera and I thought Jacko would lose much of his
fire in the hours ahead, so I didn't worry too much.
We ran straight down the river and had a comfortable
lunch at the same place as the day before, greatly missing Henry and George who had left for Valparaiso that
morning. Afterward we ran for the good places in the
heavy water, slighting the gentler rapids up above. We
caught a fish each in the long straight run and Jacko
stopped to work hard at the deep pool in the bend
below with flatfish and spoon. It was an obvious holding place for big fish and both boatmen believed good
might come of it.

Aquilera and I went on for the white-water chutes
between the gravel bars, though we traveled more slowly
now, searching the good places as we went. There is
a long likely stretch of water a little above the chutes,
quite wide and plentifully broken by big rocks. Aquilera wanted me to reach a long line across it and keep
swinging the fly back to our own bank. There was a
hard upstream wind from Lago Ranco by this time, but
I did my best for him, probably showing off a little
because he was obviously interested in the way the fly
went out and it was pleasant to be able to control things
under the awkward conditions. We picked up one nice
fish on a short follow from just above a rock, and I
worked out line again until the fly was reaching as it

had before. Then a backcast caught a willow bush. The timing was perfect: it must have been just as the line straightened behind and just as the boat dropped down with the current between oar strokes. My ten-foot rod broke cleanly, just above the top ferrule.

Aquilera was horrified, until I assured him that I had a spare top at the hotel and that I hadn't broken a top like that in twenty years (which was true) and wasn't likely to again in another twenty (which may well have been an idle boast). I couldn't find enough Spanish to tell him I thought it was a just retribution for putting on a show and also for my timidity in changing to a heavier leader after the previous day's break. But whatever the abstracts of the situation may have been, it meant that I was going to have to fish the chutes with a light dry-fly rod.

When we got down there and I studied the situation I decided I would fish a good part of the inside run, not only with the dry-fly rod, but with a floating fly. I did so and was rewarded by two nice fish.

I tried the same thing in the big run, drifting the fly along the edge of the hard water, but nothing moved to it, so I changed to the largest wet fly I felt the rod could handle properly. That got us nowhere, so I changed again to the big squirreltail I had been using with the heavy rod. It was uncomfortable to fish and very difficult to control in the wind, but I got it out there and rather quickly hooked two three-pounders which came safely to the net. Then I lost a lightly hooked fish that jumped several times and that was all the pool seemed to hold.

Jacko came through while I was looking over the

water ahead and said he was going on to fish the bar at the mouth of the river. I said we would follow pretty soon. But I was enjoying the way the little rod controlled the fish—far better and more easily than the heavier rod I had been using—even though it would not control the big fly. And I had an idea I could wade across to the shallow bar between the two streams where I had broken in the big fish the previous evening. If I could I would be able to reach some nice-looking water. It had to be by wading because Aquilera had taken the boat on down to the end of the bar and walked back to me.

There was a very fast, deep run of water close under the gravel bar we were on. I tested it with a stick for as far out as I could and judged it not quite waist deep, so I eased into it. Eased is probably the wrong word; I was more nearly swept into it and all I could do was make way across while I was making way downstream. But it worked and I came up on to the shallow with no more than a cupful in my waders.

It was really a lovely place. Ahead of me was a wide reach of sweeping current, quite flat, quite shallow except in two places that were obviously deeper channels. And the heavy run I had just crossed swung to meet it at the V-shaped end of the shallow I was standing on. I fished it down carefully, step by step, until the fly was swinging just below the point of the shallow. When the fly was within two or three yards of the end of its swing I clearly saw the following surge of a good fish. Then I felt a light touch on the fly. I left it there, holding the beat on the rod top, reaching round to give the fly a longer follow. Then I saw drag

on the line and knew the fish had taken. A moment
later he was tearing downstream.

I didn't stop to wonder about his size. I just thought
he was big and I wanted to be across the deep run and
in position to follow him. My crossing was fast and
wet and the reel was still running as I scrambled up
the steep slope of the gravel. The rest was exciting
enough at the time, when the end was uncertain and
the size of the fish still unknown, but I cannot remember anything about it that was remarkable. The fish
weighed three and a half pounds. I probably should be
glad he was no larger.

We left it at that, happily enough—five perfect rainbows, running from two and three-quarter to three and
a half pounds, all taken in wild and beautiful water
within an hour or so, represent as sharp a spell of fishing as any man should wish for. Jacko was still at the
bar when we got there and the sun had just set across
the lake. He had taken a nice fish at the bar, but he
was impatient to start for the hotel. "Don't, Jacko," I
said. "Stay for a while. It's a lovely evening."

"No," he said. "I'm going to make my scene."

"Why bother? We've had a nice enough day."

"It was very important that you should see the Hueinahue. It was all arranged until that artisan had to
show his authority. It is important the hotel people
should know and Herr Ziegler should know."

As always when Jacko was in the process of saving
honor or restoring damaged dignity, he was quite well
aware of the funny side of the situation, and his enjoyment of anything he achieved was largely humorous. As nearly as I could make out in any encounter

of his I observed, the same was true of the other side; the whole thing, in fact, was largely a matter of form, about halfway between a sport and a ceremony. But I could never get away from the fear that someone, not understanding the precise rules of the affair, might be unduly hurt. So I was sorry he had maintained his indignation long enough to stop fishing early and follow out his intent.

He left just as the sunset light was coming on the water and I watched his boat growing smaller without remembering I had a fly out. When I did remember, my line was drowned and the fly somewhere far down on the drop-off from the bar. That is never a bad situation, so I retrieved carefully, working the fly. Just as it came near the surface, about ten feet behind the boat, a great fish rolled at it, head, back and tail out of the water and catching the lovely light. He was hooked and started his fight with a majestic slowness. I had just begun to wonder how best to stir him up with the little rod when the fly came away.

Aquilera said only, "He was very big, very big."

I said, "We will find another," and made him put me out where I could wade. He went about some business of his own then and I was left alone with the river's great sweeping mouth and that glorious sunset. It grew and grew as I fished until it was, perhaps, the finest I have ever seen in my life, over the islands and the low hills west of the lake. Farthest west the sky was little horizontal lines of red, sharply marked by dark clouds. Above these was rolling layer after rolling layer of heavy red gold fleece, with a long sweep of pure gold cloud across it all, reaching up and up until it seemed vertically overhead against red and red and black and gold. All this was reflected again before me on the windless, current-twisted water of the bar, and it was all around the sky, all up the sky, until the world seemed suddenly vast under the sky and the sky itself as wide and high and deep as infinity, yet still clear to the eye.

As I watched and fished another fish rolled lazily in the red gold water and I set the hook and he went away for the depths of the lake. The little rod brought him safely back and controlled his shorter runs and I was just getting the net ready when Aquilera came plodding back and did it for me. We put the fish on the scales right there and held a match to read them, for the sunset was suddenly gone. He wouldn't weigh five pounds, no matter how I tried it. But he was a long way over two kilos.

Aquilera said, "It is too late for any more." I didn't really believe him, but I didn't want any more. So we climbed in the boat and went.

Back at the hotel Jacko had been far too successful with his scene. Herr Ziegler had said that he person-ally would fire the tugboat skipper the next day and if his joint owner made any objections he would buy him out. Our charming host and hostess were genuinely upset and Jacko himself was a little distressed by the effect he had produced. It was, I think, the first time he had come up against people who really understood fishing and really tried to produce what the fishermen wanted. I assured them I understood exactly how such a thing could happen, that it didn't matter and that I still thought Llifen the best fishing center in Chile, which was no more than the truth, though I'm not sure they believed me.

The next day, as we went down to the launch that was to take us to Puerto Nuevo, at the foot of the lake, Herr Ziegler reiterated his intention of firing the tugboat captain, with considerable emphasis. I suggested that this was altogether too drastic, but he assured me that such people must be taught their place. There could be no softness with them.

As we walked on Jacko grinned happily to himself. "He is ruthless, that man. A regular dictator. The captain will be very sorry."

"You really think he'll fire him?" I asked. "He seemed like a pretty good skipper and they must be fairly hard to find."

"No," Jacko said. "He will be very, very angry with him, but in the end he will not fire him. He will relent."

Big Fish Story

Puerto Nuevo is at the opposite end of Lago Ranco from Llifen, a little frame-built hotel above a sloping beach about a mile from the lake's outlet into Rio Bueno. Carlos Dippel, the proprietor, is a tall, very handsome man of German extraction, though as dark and volatile as a Spaniard. He is a most courteous and delightful host and takes a very keen interest in the fishing.

We arrived soon after noon on a Sunday. Half a dozen attractive girls in very tight, very smooth swimming suits were decorating the beach. All the girls were brown, but it seemed to me every suit was a different color—I had noticed red, white, black, blue and yellow, when Jacko said, "It is a waste of time to look. They are not staying in the hotel. They are here from La Union because it is Sunday." I wondered how he knew.

Later when we went into the little dining room for lunch, several of the girls were in a party at a nearby table. After a little while Jacko told me, "Three are married. The other two are younger sisters of two of the married ones and they would like to be married. Those are the most dangerous kind."

Again I wondered how he knew. It wasn't impossible to figure out the married ones—one of them even had a small child sitting beside her. But I couldn't assign the sisters with any degree of certainty. I asked Jacko how he knew. "It is quite clear," he said.

The room was an interesting one. It held an assortment of tables under clean white cloths and every corner and space was filled with some bright decoration or bric-a-brac. There were silver cups and polished glasses, a great brass shell case holding plumes of pampas grass, mirrors on every wall, vases of bright flowers on every table. On one wall were two great Bavarian engravings, appropriately scenes of sportsmen returning to wayside inns. On the other walls were fallow deer hides and horns, from a herd that had been naturalized on one of the islands in the lake, and an assortment of pennants celebrating everything from the Cu-

erpo de Carabineros de Chile to the Hotel Burnier in
Osorno. Every flat surface that wasn't otherwise occu-
pied held a bowl or vase of flowers.

But the most impressive thing in the whole room was
what I at first took to be a fireplace with a huge man-
telpiece. A second glance revealed it as a settee, but a
settee the like of which I had never seen before. The
seat and back were stiffly upholstered in heavy tapestry
with a pattern not unlike that of a Turkish carpet. The
seat itself was not especially wide, but had imposingly
carved wings and arms that broadened the base for the
mass above. There *was* a mantel—or a shelf that went
clear across above the back of the seat and which supported everything from massive silver cups and pottery
beer steins to bowls of flowers and china dogs. Above
this was an enormous mirror, framed by many intricately
carved little shelves, each carrying its share of bric-a-
brac, and above the mirror was more carving, turrets
and embrasures and castellates reaching almost to the
ceiling.

In front of the settee was a round table, set with a
single place and almost equally imposing. Silver gleamed
in ranks upon the white cloth—as, I should say in fair-
ness, it gleamed on all the other tables. A great silver
bowl of flowers was the centerpiece. A bottle of white
wine, a bottle of red wine and a bottle of mineral water
stood beside it, each decorated by a little garland of
porcelain flowers. A porcelain ash tray and cruet stand
matched these garlands and a silver hand bell beside a
cigar box completed the still life. It seemed obvious that
all this was for someone of importance and I asked
Jacko about it.

"It is for Mr. Featherstone," Jacko said. "He is an Englishman who has lived many years in Chile and comes here every year for the whole summer. You must meet him."

"Is he a fisherman?" I asked.

Jacko nodded. "They say he does not fish as much as he used to, but he ties many flies."

Late in the afternoon I took a boat and boatman and went down to the outlet of the big lake. There was no one else down there and I told the boatman I wanted to go ashore and fish the first two or three pools of the river.

The lake broke beautifully over its bar, foaming into a short turbulent pool that swung almost at a right angle to cascade into another pool, long, deep, swift and imposing between rocky canyon walls. I wanted to fish the first pool, but the boatman shook his head and took me down to the second. Just at the head I could work it with the fly and a good fish of three and a half pounds took almost at once, right below the fall. After that I could find nothing and the eddy on my side quickly became too deep to wade and too wide to cast across with any satisfaction.

I had put a small bait-casting rod in the boat and the boatman had brought it along with him, so I took it and began reaching out across the eddy with a spoon, confidently expecting to hit into a big fish. I fished the whole of that long pool quite thoroughly, changing from spoon to devon minnow and back to spoon again. Once or twice I saw trout of fair size follow the bait around into the eddy. Once a rather dark fish of about three pounds followed almost to my feet and struck twice—at the half-ounce lead I had set two or three feet ahead of the spoon, not at the spoon itself. And that was all from the long pool, though I tried the fly again at the head.

The boatman wanted to go back and fish the bar from the boat, but I told him I would fish the first pool before we did that. He followed me down without enthusiasm and I found a place where I could wade out quite comfortably beside the rush of water at the head of the pool. I made a short cast or two into a little run of white water beside the big tumbling rapid, letting out line, and the fly was taken fiercely in midcurrent by a fish of two pounds. I looked for the boatman, who had the net, and saw that he had wandered off downstream with my casting rod and was working the spoon from a high ledge of rock. I yelled and he came back and netted the fish for me.

That was the only small fish I had from that first pool. A few moments later, when I still had only forty or fifty feet of line reaching out into the main current, a three-and-a-half-pounder took the fly right on top, again in the middle of the white water. The boatman was away, fishing on his own again, evidently quite convinced that I should find nothing else in the pool. There was plenty of time for him to get back. My fish took full advantage of the race of current and ran me almost to the lip of the fall below the pool. I made no attempt to hold him and he came back on his own, very deep down. When the boatman got to me with the net I was standing precariously at the edge of what seemed to be a shelf of conglomerate, looking down into at least twenty feet of water that raced in a back eddy from the main run. My fish was somewhere near the bottom of it. When I brought him up he thrashed heavily and jumped twice, but I held him out of the current and we netted him safely.

I went back to where I had hooked the fish, got out line again and soon had another of exactly the same size a few yards farther down the run. This fish had followed and missed my fly on two successive casts through the heavy water before I could slow it enough to let him have it, but otherwise he behaved exactly like his predecessor. The boatman had also repeated his performance of wandering off and had to be brought back by a yell. But this time he stayed with me after netting the fish. I believe he was beginning to think the pool might have something in it.

As though to justify whatever doubts he had left I fished on down as far as I could wade with only one pull from a fish that would not come again. So I began putting out more line, until I was working just about all I could throw. Nothing took. I threw straight across, then stripped off two more yards and let the current pull them out. Almost as the fly started its swing I could see a big fish shouldering through the white water behind it. He was probably three feet behind, swimming like a porpoise, right on top, and seeming to gain scarcely at all. Be he must have gained because he hit with a tremendous pull and was away before I could get the rod up. He also came to the net in the end—an ounce or less under four pounds and hooked deep in the gullet, as deeply, I think, as I have ever hooked a fish on a fly.

After that, which was about the most exciting half-hour of trout fishing I can remember, I was willing to settle for the smooth quiet water of the bar in the last of the evening light. It looked like very good water indeed and the boatman insisted on putting out a small flatfish to troll on my casting rod while I fished the same big fly I had used in the pool—a Chilean fly called the Campeone, which had a red hackle and tail, a green seal's fur body and wings of light mallard strips with long streamers of bronze peacock herl. The flatfish caught a nice little rainbow of one and a half pounds, which I released. The Campeone caught another three-and-a-half-pounder, which I kept. So we went home with five three-pounders, one of them almost four, and a little fish of two and a half pounds that looked lost among them. They were all beautiful fish, nearly all maiden three-year-olds as the scales later showed, and they were all feeding on apancora and grasshoppers. Which creature they supposed they had in the Campeone I do not know.

At dinner we saw Mr. Featherstone at his table. He was a neatly dressed, spare, mustached, handsome man of about sixty, and he sat on his imposing settee with unself-conscious dignity. When he came into the room he did not, as nearly everyone does in small Chilean hotels, look up to wish us good evening. Nor did he show, by any least sign during the whole of his meal, that he was aware of anyone else in the room except the maid who was serving him. With her he had several passages of lively conversation and evidently a shared joke or two because he laughed quite heartily once or twice.

When his meal was finished he sat back with a big cup of coffee and lit a cigar. Almost immediately a young Chilean, dressed in his best blue serge, came in with a chess board, opened it on the table and set up the pieces, all in complete silence. Still in silence and rather quickly, the game was played. Mr. Featherstone won. He explained one or two details of the game to the young Chilean, laughing over them in a way that clearly showed he was instructing. Then the young man stood up, wished him a respectful good night and went out of the room. A few minutes later, without a glance to right or left, Mr. Featherstone followed him.

I was interested and unwisely admitted my interest to Jacko. "The boatman says he hardly ever goes fishing," I told him, "except in November and December. Now he just ties flies and gives them away. I wonder what they are like."

"Don't worry," Jacko said. "He will show you. He will want to meet you."

"I doubt that. If ever I saw a man who didn't want to be bothered by anyone it's Mr. Featherstone."

"Don't worry," Jacko said again. "He will show you his flies."

I saw the onset of another affair of honor. "For God's sake don't go and bother him," I begged. "He's entitled to his privacy."

"Of course not. He will want to meet you when he knows who you are. He will be much impressed by those fish you caught tonight."

We were away early next morning for Rio Bueno and did not see Mr. Featherstone. Jacko was delighted to be fishing the river again and was certain we should find a big fish. With the temperature of lake and river around 67° F I was much less optimistic.

We started at the first huge, lake-like pool below the canyon—a few boats have been upset in the rapids of the canyon itself and the run is no longer attempted. There were some good fish in that first pool, a few of which followed the fly, but they were lazy and did not take. From there down the river is mainly a big boat river, with even gliding current except where a smooth, powerful slick sweeps over into the head of each new pool. I found these were very strong and difficult to wade, but I did my best with them and by lunchtime had half a dozen fish, all bright gleaming rainbows, up to three pounds. Jacko had an almost identical catch except that his biggest was a brown trout.

We had lunch on a lovely slope of bright, grasslike moss and small green leaves, opposite a great pool that swept in an easy curve under the far bank. After lunch Jacko said to his boatman, who was quite an old man, "Where can the caballero find a very big fish?"

The old man pointed to the pool in front of us. "Here, in December, Don Fernando has a brown trout of five kilos. On a spoon."

"Go and catch his brother," Jacko told me.

I grinned and went, wondering how many similarly forlorn hopes I had chased in Chile, and how much more of the wonderful fishing for three- and four-pounders I might have had if it hadn't been for the everlasting search.

The pool was a narrow run of good current, about twenty feet deep among a maze of sunken trees. There was a great, wide eddy, gradually sloping into the deep current from our grassy bank, so it had to be fished from the boat. I made a few casts at the head, then let the fly hang as the boatman eased slowly down.

The strike—it couldn't possibly be called a rise—was

slow and very deep, but the fish ran at once. He ran
with complete authority, taking my whole fly line under
water and the backing splice and several yards of backing. I was pretty well resigned to the idea of trouble
with the tree trunks, but by some miracle I brought
him freely back from the run. He ran again, twice, in
almost exactly the same way, taking about the same
length of line and burying the whole fly line. Neither
run could be checked and each time I felt sure he would
twist under something and break away. But each time
he came back, and the second time he was very tired.

I told the boatman to work slowly across the eddy,
so that I could beach the fish on the smooth slope of
sand just below where Jacko and his boatman were
watching us. He started and the fish followed. I felt
sorry for the fish. All my tackle was tested and sound,
the pool favored him not at all once he was away from
the sunken logs and he hadn't a chance. I saw him first
as a huge white mouth, following about thirty feet behind the boat and probably ten feet down in the water.
Then I could see a long brown shape behind the white
mouth. I took in line gently and easily until the loop
of my leader was just under water.

"Five kilos," I told the boatman.

He stood up to look over my shoulder. "No," he said.
"Six or seven kilos. Seven."

Jacko was dancing on the beach. The old boatman
was standing there with him. The nose of my boat
touched gently. I glanced over the side, all ready to step
out and finish the thing. Then the fly came away. My
boatman swore. The old boatman swore. Jacko sat down
on the beach with his head in his hands. As a matter of

routine, I pulled the fly in and checked it. The point of the hook had broken off at the barb.

I stripped a little line off the reel and flipped the fly over beside Jacko. "Look," I told him.

He sat holding the fly in his hands, as though he could not believe what he saw. "You mean the hook broke off? For no reason at all? It is an outrage. You must write about it and name the maker so that he will be disgraced all over the world. Who was the maker?"

"I don't know," I said. "But it is a thing that happens sometimes. Too much temper, I guess."

"But you must know. Where did you get the fly? At least you must write to the store and they will make a scene with the maker." He let the fly go in disgust. I brought it back to me and began to take it off the leader.

"I didn't buy it," I said. "Someone gave it to me."

"That is terrible," Jacko said. "What are you going to do with it?"

"Throw it away." I had it loose from the leader and was about to do just that.

"Give it to me," Jacko said. "I will keep it and show it everywhere."

I gave him the offending fly and he put it carefully in his wallet.

I suppose the rest of the day should have been an anticlimax, yet many good and many interesting things happened. The fishing was quiet; we each caught half a dozen more fish during the afternoon, of much the same size as those we had had at noon. But the smooth, gliding power of the river was always impressive and I was tempted again and again to wade beyond where I should have, until the shifting of gravel under my feet warned me that the weight of water against my body was too great and I had to edge back or go swimming. It was big fish water all the way and I was constantly hopeful that I would hook into another monster and make amends for the broken fly.

Once we saw a big fish, a great thick-bodied brown trout that jumped clear out of the water about fifty feet behind the boat. I covered him instantly, but without much hope—I had seen the boat of a local fisherman pull into the bank about a hundred yards downstream. The fish jumped again and again I gave him the fly instantly. Then I told my boatman, "He's been hooked," and pointed to the boat below us. We went down to it and the fisherman had just finished tying another lure to his hand line. He couldn't wait to tell us of the enormous trout that had broken away with his homemade flatfish. The poor man had all my sympathy. He was a genuine enthusiast, anxious to show us just what he had been using, still breathless with the memory of the great fish that had seemed to be his.

A little farther downstream we came upon another fisherman, a furtive man with a short length of gill net strung ineffectively along the shore and rather badly tangled in bushes and roots. He would not look up as we passed and my boatman kept well over from him.

The river split into several channels and took us down among dark, wild-looking islands, with ragged dark green trees from which bandurrias called in lost and broken voices. The little night herons were everywhere, perched on rocks, on slanting tree trunks, high in the trees. They scarcely moved from the boat, flapping a few yards to perch again and look back at us over hunched shoulders. There were some wonderful pools in this stretch, dark swirling waters perfectly designed to grow and hold enormous brown trout. I did catch a brown of three pounds somewhere among them and lose another of the same size, but those are the only fish I can remember.

So we came to the ferry at Puerto Lapiz, where Carlos Dippel was to meet us with his Studebaker truck. It was already dusk under the cloudy sky, and the ferry was crossing to the far side where a party of brightly dressed horsemen and horsewomen waited for it, larking with their horses and raising dust clouds. They were obviously in fine spirits.

We landed and began to take down our gear. Watching the party as it boarded the ferry, Jacko said, "They are returning from a fiesta. From a religious festival. They are very drunk."

As the ferry reached our bank I saw that the girls of the party were young and pretty as well as colorfully dressed. They had dismounted to go aboard the ferry, as had a few of the men. When the ferry landed there was the ceremony of remounting. This was a splendid opportunity for strategically located pinches, an opportunity by no means disregarded. Its acceptance was made evident by sharp, but quite musical squeals and some resounding slaps. The unattached males of the party had thundered off the ferry and up the hill at full gallop. As each couple became organized in the saddle, it did the same. The last man dropped his poncho as he whirled to follow his lady. Jacko picked it up and handed it to him. "Gracias, señor," he said, and lifted his sombrero. Then he was away.

Carlos came soon after and we drove home with him through the stormy evening, passing the scattered cavalcade of celebrants on the way. Jacko had told Carlos of the net fisherman and he was intensely indignant. By chance we met two carabineros traveling in the opposite direction. Carlos stopped the truck instantly and told them the story with great excitement, and they promised to investigate.

At dinner that night, I learned why Jacko had wanted the fly. He produced it for Carlos Dippel, who had already heard the story at length, and told him the story again. Carlos managed suitable expressions of surprise, wonder and indignation, then went promptly to Mr. Featherstone's table and repeated the story to him.

Mr. Featherstone took the fly and turned it over and over, very slowly as he listened. He was smiling gently, by no means without proper sympathy and interest. As Carlos finished, Mr. Featherstone gently pulled a few hairs from the wing of the fly and handed it back. He said nothing at all. That was as close as I came to meeting Mr. Featherstone, but I had to admit to Jacko that he was a sound fly-tier. All the flies I had of that pattern were poorly tied, without sufficient wax to hold the hairs firmly to the hook.

A Restful Place

Jacko had told me many times, "you will like the Petrohue. It is your kind of river, a wading river, much too fast for boats." He was right. I think the Petrohue was the finest river I fished in Chile.

We made a considerable journey from Puerto Nuevo

to get there, passing many rivers I should have liked to have fished if I had had more time: the Golgol, a wading river that flows into Puyehue Lake, the Pilmaiquen, a boat river which drains the same lake, the Rahue, another fine river near Osorno, and others whose names I forget. All hold plenty of trout, and big trout. One knowledgeable spoon-fisherman I met at Puerto Nuevo told me he caught a trout of nine kilos in the Rahue and his friend had one of six kilos the same day.

We went by taxi from Puerto Nuevo to Osorno, a distance of about fifty miles, crossing the Pilmaiquen on the way and passing through a lovely country of rolling, easy hills with horsemen and little pigs and wandering geese along the roads, lichen-covered gates and fences, big farm fields in fallow or pasture with tall forest trees left to stand nobly in them.

Osorno is a most attractive city of about thirty thousand, the largest center in southern Chile. We had time to stop for lunch at the Hotel Burnier, which looks out over the beautifully kept Plaza with its long rectangular pool and well-planned planting. The hotel was absolutely first class and we found ourselves in a delightful modern dining room, filled with animated, well-dressed people. The food was at least as good as the setting, perfectly served, and with a bottle of Rhin Undurraga and an adequate tip our meal cost just three hundred pesos—at that time a few cents over three dollars. I thought the hotel generally similar in quality to the Frontera in Temuco, and with several good rivers nearby a fisherman could spend a very comfortable week or two there.

After lunch we found a small exhibition of forty or fifty Chilean paintings in the hotel. Many were of Lago

Ranco and other places we had seen and a few were finely done, realistic scenes that still gave an interpretation of the country through its volcanos and rocky headlands and fine trees and stormy days. But I was surprised to find that Canadian painters, dealing with similar material, are not only more sophisticated and advanced technically, but far more profound in feeling. Perhaps it is unfair to reach such a conclusion on the basis of a single provincial exhibition, but Jacko assured me that one or two of the artists represented in the show are very highly regarded in Chile.

We caught an afternoon train from Osorno to Puerto Varas, at the foot of Lago Llanquihue, the largest lake in Chile. There we found ourselves in another immense railway hotel, even more luxurious than the one at Pucon. We took to its luxuries happily, washing away the dirt of the train journey in the superb bathrooms, eating a magnificent dinner in the dining room and watching a gay mixture of Chileans and Argentines—for Puerto Varas is on the main southern route between the two countries—dancing to an excellent orchestra.

But Puerto Varas was only an overnight stop for us. We picked up mail there which told us that my friend Lee Richardson, of Seattle, would join us on the Petrohue to make a motion picture for the airline. And we had time the next morning to look out over the wide blue lake and see five white-coned volcanos against the sky—Puntiagudo, at the head of Lago Rupanco, Osorno, the nearest and our constant familiar companion for the next several days, Tronador, immense and distant on the Argentine border, Calbuco, on the south shore of the lake, and one other whose name I forget. They were deeply impressive and I recognized in the long, sweeping slopes and perfect white cone of Osorno the loveliest and most satisfying volcano I had ever seen.

We left Puerto Varas soon after breakfast to travel by bus along the lake shore to the little German hotel near the Petrohue River, where Lee was to meet us. As we settled into the hotel I was shocked by an air of ruthless, disciplined efficiency about the place—it was evident in notices on the walls, in clerks, chambermaids, waitresses, everyone we saw—and by an unnatural silence. Thinking to counteract the gloomy impression, I asked Jacko where the bar was, and was still more deeply shocked.

"There is none," he said. "This is a place where very heavy German families come to rest and eat and grow heavier. They eat very much and whenever they are not eating they are resting. There is no levity at all. It is not a Chilean place."

Nor, it seemed, was it a fisherman's place. No one had any suggestions about the river, how to get to it, where to fish it, how to find a guide or even a small boy to carry our gear. If it hadn't been that Lee was to meet us there I think I would have moved out at once. As it was we managed to get a ride on a sight-seeing bus that was going along the river, and left with strict orders to be back for dinner at 8:00 P.M. or go hungry to bed.

We got off the bus with the tourists and looked at the falls. Knowing nothing of the river, it seemed to us as good a place to start as any, so we let them leave us there. Someone at the hotel had mentioned it might be possible to find a small boy at a farmhouse near the falls;

we found the house and were greeted by a bevy of fine dogs that looked like golden Labradors and seemed not at all used to strangers. A man appeared from somewhere in the house, but he knew nothing of a small boy and nothing of how to get at the river. I told Jacko to ask him what he kept the dogs for. For protection, he said, to keep pumas and people away.

As we came up in the bus I had noticed several places where wide, clear, volcanic washes ran down from the road to the river, so I suggested that we walk back to one of them and follow it down. We came to a fine pool, but were disappointed to find the river quite milky with silt, especially on our side.

We put in a fairly hard afternoon of exploration. The river was very fine, big, fast and broken, with some noble pools, but its banks were rocky and hard to travel. I kept changing flies, hoping to find something that would show up in the thick water and after an hour or more I rose one good fish to a Gray Ghost, missed him, rose him again, hooked him and lost him. Jacko was very disgusted with the whole affair. He had rheumatism, a leaky boot, a broken landing net and no safety swivels for his spoons. He said he would lie down in the sun and sleep while I went on with my exploration.

I stayed with it, becoming more and more impressed with the river, though I managed to rise only a few small fish. The water was warmer than I had hoped it would be—65° F—but I felt fairly certain the cloudiness was due to a recent storm and would pass quite quickly. At one point as we walked down the road I had noticed what looked like a pool of clear water down near the river, but when I asked Jacko about it he said he remembered it from a previous visit and it held only very small trout. I was inclined to go back there and take a look, but by the time I got to where I had left Jacko it was nearly seven-thirty, time to go back to the road and wait for the bus on its return trip. It was cold when the sun went down, so we began to walk. At eight-thirty the bus caught up to us. Fortunately, it had other passengers, so the hotel relaxed its rule and gave us all dinner.

Lee didn't arrive that night, but a wire the next morning said he would be in the following night. I suggested to Jacko that we should take the bus right through to Lago Todos Los Santos, the source of the Petrohue, in the hope of getting above the clouded water. On the way we crossed a little stream, the Maquina, which was bringing down very dirty water, though not much of it at that time of the morning. By afternoon, with the sun full on the glacier, it would be running much harder.

We found a very pleasant little hotel at the foot of the lake and I was able to hire a boat there to go out after plankton samples and temperature readings. The lake itself was magnificent, long and narrow between timbered shores and splendid mountains, its water a deep turquoise blue from the reflection of billions of silt particles brought down into it from the glaciers of the high volcanos.

I had to go some little distance to get depth for temperature readings, so there was not much time to fish before lunch, though I tried a little along the reedy banks of the narrow arm that leads down to the river, and rose one fish.

At lunchtime the little hotel, normally so peaceful between the slope of the volcano and the edge of the lake, became a scene of bustling activity. Two bus loads of passengers arrived from Puerto Varas, on their way through to Argentina. At the same time the little steamer *Esmeralda* docked at the wharf from its run down the lake and unloaded a similar number of passengers bound in the opposite direction. Both groups crowded into the hotel dining room for lunch, while baggage was transferred from bus to steamer and steamer to bus. Jacko met a very charming cousin returning from Argentina and we had an excellent lunch with her and her husband.

After lunch I was lucky to meet Pancho Jones of Lima, a keen fisherman who spends several weeks at Petrohue every season. He had read one or two of my books and was generous with some extremely sound information. He said he fished a good deal from a boat anchored in the current just above the outlet of the lake and that he caught some good fish there, including some that he believed to be salmon up to ten and twelve pounds. This was the first local mention of salmon I had heard in Chile, though I had checked everywhere, especially on the San Pedro where Pacific salmon were once rumored to have established, and I was very curious about it.

We found two boats and two boatmen—mine was a bright little black-eyed boy of twelve or fourteen—and rowed down to the outlet. My boy anchored the boat just over the first little run of current and I fished from there while Jacko trolled nearby. He soon had a fine, silvery, three-pound rainbow. I reached all the water I could from our anchorage, then had the boy drop down to the head of a rocky island that divided the first two rapids of the river. There I got out on my feet.

I fished the smaller run first, which died rather quickly into a slackish pool. Several good fish rose to my fly there and others followed it, but I missed them all and decided to go to the big rapid on the other side of the island, though it looked a formidable place to wade.

The wading was far better than I had expected. The water was very fast and quite deep, but the rocks under it had a mossy covering that gave a very good grip, and at the head of the rapid they were on a slight slope against the stream, so that the weight of the current held me down in a pleasantly secure way.

I threw right into the white water at the head of the run and a thick, four-pound rainbow made a nice lazy jump, clear out, with the fly in his mouth. I waited a moment, then struck, and he was away at once, down and across the current, jumping steadily for seventy or eighty yards.

We brought him back out of there somehow and finally got him safely netted. My little guide's black eyes were sparkling and he was breathing hard with excitement and the effort of straddling two rocks to net the fish. "Get another one, señor," he said.

So I worked back in at the same place and as soon as I was covering new water I hooked another fine fish, only a three-pounder this time, but a powerful runner and jumper just the same.

After that I spent a difficult hour working my way down the rapid, through the pool and into the head of the next pool, but found nothing more. The water was waist deep there and about as fast as I cared to wade, so I came back to the head of the first pool again and worked still farther out. As soon as my fly reached farther over into the white water than it had before, it was taken by a three-pounder. "Another," said my little boy. I went still farther out and cast still farther. A four-pounder came racing across the surface behind the swing of the fly, grabbed it and was hooked. "Another," said the little boy as he landed it. And I got another, the best fish of all, a four-and-a-half-pounder that ran twice almost clear across the wide stretch of broken water and jumped three or four times on each run.

That ended it. I believe I did wade a little farther out and cast a little farther, but the magic was gone from the pool or my fly or the little boy's enraptured chant. I was happy enough. It was the first pool of Rio Bueno over again, but with bigger fish, stronger fish and more of them. I don't think I have ever caught better-conditioned rainbows than those were or fished more exciting water.

When we got to the hotel Lee was waiting there for us, comfortably settled in but completely exhausted by the long journey; from Seattle to Santiago by air, then by train to Osorno and by taxi from there, without a real stop anywhere. The sight of our fish cheered him a lot and strangely enough the hotel management was equally delighted. They even placed the catch on display on the floor of the front veranda. The clientele was a little more doubtful. When I came out after dinner I found a broad-based, tweed-skirted German lady poking a powerful leather shoe at my lovely catch. "Fish," she said, with enormous disapproval. "Fish. And blood." Her eyes swept her resting compatriots on the veranda in search of sympathy, and I withdrew quietly. I felt I was living up to the motto of the hotel, hanging in printed cards on every wall: *Silencio de cada uno asegura el reposo de todos*, the silence of each one ensures the peace of everyone or, more freely, one corpse makes a whole cemetery.

The Beach of the Deer

EVEN THOUGH I KNEW I WOULD SEE him again in Santiago within a month, it was a sad thing to say good-by to Jacko and put him on the bus for Puerto Varas next morning. No one can ever have traveled with a more patient or more faithful friend or fished with a more generous and cheerful fisherman.

Lee and I left almost immediately for the little hotel at Petrohue, where I hoped to stay for several days and get him some good pictures of Chilean trout fishing. We arrived at the hotel, bought a beer and settled ourselves in the sunlight to talk fishing with Pancho Jones. I asked Pancho about a clear pool I had seen from the road and he said that he had caught only a few little red-spotted trout from it—he thought it was the small branch of the main river that cuts off by the falls. As we were talking, a very powerfully built, dark man, wearing Tyrolean leather shorts and a bright shirt, came up and introduced himself as Agustin Edwards. "I've been wiring and writing all over the country," he said, "trying to catch up with you. You're going to be around for a few days. Come on to my place and stay there.

It's only two or three miles up the lake, so you'll be quite close enough to the fishing."

I had heard of Don Agustin, as nearly everyone who goes to Chile is bound to hear of him, and I was delighted to meet him. I had also wanted to stay at the little hotel at Petrohue, but he would have none of that and within a few minutes Lee and I had loaded our stuff aboard his launch, the *Puma*, and were speeding up the lake.

Agustin's Lodge, Playa Venado or the Beach of the Deer, is two or three hundred feet up on a hillside, on the south side of the lake, and its windows look straight across the blue-green water to the magnificence of Osorno. I had been almost constantly aware of the mountain ever since coming to the Petrohue, but from Playa Venado it is inescapable, a superb mountain, far enough away to be fully seen, close enough to seem the biggest thing in the world. The maps say it is only nine thousand feet, but it stands all by itself, a mountain rising from the plain on an enormous circular base, fifty miles in diameter. The lower slopes are dark and even, marked by gleaming runnels from the glaciers. The snow crown, starting at four thousand feet, carries the line of the slopes smoothly and evenly on to the domed summit. The whole effect is mass in repose, unchanging in loveliness though constantly changed by the sweep and shape of cloud forms, by light and shade, by moonlight or sunlight or the seasons. The mountain has been in repose now for over ninety years, yet no one can say it will not some day burst into eruption again; in this also is part of its character and fascination.

Playa Venado commands much of the lake, as well as the mountain, yet it is so set into the hillside, and so

tiny in the scale of the country that one could pass two
or three hundred yards out from shore without seeing
it among the trees. It was a strange and satisfying place
to belong to, even temporarily, and it added enormously
to the pleasure of the next four or five days we spent
on the Petrohue as, in greater degree, did Don Agustin
himself.

I chose to go early to look at the clear pool I had seen
from the road. Agustin had told us of a good pool in
the main river and when we drove down to it we found
that the two were one and the same thing—or rather,
that the outlet of the pool I had seen entered the main
river at the head of Agustin's pool. In spite of my in-
stinctive feeling for the clear-water pool, I was very
slow to understand it. It was really a broadening of the
little stream or arm, which passed smoothly along both
sides of a grassy island before tumbling a hundred yards
or so through a series of little rapids to the river. As
soon as I saw it closely I told Lee, "It looks exactly like
a chalkstream." But it was already evening and there
was not too much time for fishing, so we went on to
the big pool in the main river.

In the big pool, just below the entrance of the clear
stream, I immediately caught a brown trout of five
pounds on a Campeone. It was a very pale, silvery fish,
with no red spots and only faint halos around its black
spots and it was in superb condition, less than twenty-
one inches long; yet it undoubtedly was a brown trout.
I followed it by another very similar fish of three and
three-quarter pounds, another of two and a half and a
rainbow of two and a quarter. Farther down the pool

I could get only reluctant plucks from fish I could not hook.

As we passed the clear-water pool on the way back to the truck in the dusk, it looked more than ever like a chalkstream and dry fly water. There were even fish rising—small fish, I supposed, secure in the satisfaction of the big fish I was carrying. The clearness of the water puzzled me, because the Petrohue itself carries the blue silt of the lake even at its clearest. I asked Agustin if he had ever followed the clear stream down from the falls, whether it could pass somewhere underground through gravel and clear itself. He said he had not, but that no stream except the muddy little Maquina crossed the road between the lake and where we were, so presumably it had to be a branch of the main stream.

The next day Lee and I took my bright little black-eyed boy and another youngster from the hotel to carry our gear, and went out after pictures. It was a lovely day and we fished several grand, fast-water pools which yielded me only a couple of two and a half pound rainbows and even those were reluctant fish that took a slow fly worked in the back eddies. But there was fuchsia and ulmo at height of bloom, stirred by the wind, to work Lee's cameras, and I was able to show him the torrent ducks and a spotted sandpiper that might have come south from British Columbia, and some of my other Chilean wonders.

The camera had to have fish though, as well as sunlight and flowers, so it seemed only sensible to go down to where the fish had been taking the night before. I warned Lee that they might not be taking the same way under the bright afternoon sun, but they were and we showed the camera two brown trout and three rainbows, all two- and three-pounders and all in quick succession. Then things slowed down and I fished for two or three hundred yards down the pool without persuading anything to take secure hold on the fly.

This convinced my slow mind that the clear-water stream had something to do with the fish taking, so I wandered musingly back there and began to search the rocks at the mouth of the stream for May fly and sedge larvae and whatever other trout food might be there. Almost immediately I knew the answer. My hands in the water were cold; I could even feel it on the legs of my waders. I tried the thermometer and it dropped swiftly back to 51° F, a full 16° colder than the Petrohue itself. The source of the clear stream wasn't the Petrohue at all; it could only be in some upwelling spring fed underground from the glaciers of Osorno. I told Lee, "I'll bet half the fish in the river are hanging around here. I bet they're huddled along the bottom in droves wherever the line of that cold current runs under the main river."

Lee had his pictures for the day and had just about finished sorting out his cameras. "Sounds good," he said. "Do you think we could catch some more?"

"Go and try it," I told him. And within ten or fifteen minutes he had two four-pound brown trout on the bank.

By this time my thoughts were back on that chalkstream pool by the grassy island. If fish would lie in such numbers off the mouth of the stream it seemed certain that some would work up into it to feed, especially in the evenings. I greased a dry-fly line, put up a 3x leader and picked out a McKenzie yellow caddis, then walked up to the pool.

Fish were rising, but they looked to be small and I was prepared to accept disappointment. I covered the first two rises carelessly, got a slight drag on the fly and refusals. Then I hooked a brown trout of about ten inches and I was ready to believe that Pancho Jones was right. Then, up toward the head of the island, I saw the tail of a nymphing fish and I knew he was at least a three-pounder.

The moment was as breathless as only chalkstream moments are likely to be; it offered all the possibilities of devastating error that chalkstreams so commonly present, and I was already deliberately planning at least one error that might be devastating. The tail of the nymphing fish showed again, then another tail, just as big, a few feet above him. It was suddenly obvious that the bulging rise-forms of the fish showing nearer to me were also those of nymphing fish. There was a hatch of cinnamon sedges above the water, but I could see none on the water. Yet I wanted the clear distinction between dry fly and wet when I caught my fish; I did not want to compromise on the sunk nymph, even though cast upstream and drifted over the fish. So I kept to my dry fly.

I was watching the rises closely now, trying to detect a big fish under them. I could have gone up to try for the two big tails, of course, but I was afraid of scaring up the fish below and disturbing them. There was one rise, much like all the others, but more persistent, two or three yards up from the tail of the grassy island and very close under it. I put the fly there, it was taken in a nice quiet dimple and I tightened. That was the end of quietness. The fish came back downstream so fast that the line hissed with a high little bow wave along the island and across to the far bank. I thought he was headed for the rapids, but he jumped instead, then ran to my feet and back across the pool again. I worked him as hard as the 3x gut would let me, because I wanted to go after the other fish, but he was strong and an unpredictable jumper, so it took time. When I netted him he looked so big that I wasted a few more seconds in weighing him—a four-and-a-half-pound rainbow.

By the time I was fishing again the sun had gone and there was a lovely late light on the water. The two great tails were still showing from time to time, in the same lies, and I decided to try them.

The first fish refused my fly on three drifts, but each time I saw his tail break water almost as the fly reached him, so I knew he was too busy for it. I thought of changing to a nymph, decided it was too late and put the dry fly over again.

This time he took it, in the delightfully offhand manner of a fish that is busily feeding and completely unsuspicious. When I tightened he did exactly what I was afraid of—ran straight up through the shallow water, right past the other big tail. But the tail showed again, in calm unconcern, while he was still running, and I worked over to my own bank and brought him gently down again. It was nearly dark when I netted him, but the glassy surface of the water reflected all the light there was and I could see the other fish well enough to cover him. He took the first float and Lee netted him for me five minutes later—a brown trout of three and a half pounds, beautifully marked and almost an exact twin of the previous fish. The Test could have done no better.

The chalkstream, as we called it after that, was a good discovery and made me feel fine. It also confirmed the experience at the mouth of the Pirinel and my whole theory that most Chilean trout streams are too warm for the best of fishing in January and February. Agustin and I went back to the stream an evening or two later and explored it for half a mile or so, finding long flat reaches, wide and deep with little current movement, heavily brushed banks and a few fish all the way along, some of them up to four pounds or more. We did not find the source of the stream, but it cannot be very far away and I imagine Agustin has found it by now.

A day or so after we found the chalkstream, Agustin suggested that Lee and I should go up Cayutue arm to try the Cayutue River, which is a cold stream, and Calbutue Lake, which it drains. The arm is several miles long and we ran up there in the *Puma*, stopping to explore a tiny lake, cupped in a hollow a few feet above the main lake, on the way.

It was a lovely sunlit day and I noticed, as we landed by the little lake, that the underside of the big gulls soaring over the treetops reflected the blue of the lake so strongly that it was hard to believe they were not actually blue themselves. I was watching them when Lee jumped on to the rocky shore from the bow of the *Puma* and fell heavily. He was carrying his cameras and in protecting them he took the force of the fall on his face and body; his face was cut in several places and the wind was knocked out of him; what else we did not know. But he sorted himself out and we got the blood checked and he found that his cameras were un-damaged, so he soon felt cheerful enough to go on.

The Cayutue was as cold as Agustin had promised—50° F—but it is a very tiny stream, with a high fall a little way from the mouth. We climbed above the falls, where I quickly caught and released some nice little brown trout of about three-quarters of a pound. Then, with considerable difficulty, we climbed down along the falls to the big canyon pools at the foot of them, deep, narrow places and obviously fine holding water, though they seemed completely empty at that time. I should like to fish them at some time when the big fish are up from Todos Los Santos Lake, because there can be little doubt they do come in at times.

We decided to have lunch before attempting the four-mile walk to the lake. During lunch Lee's elation at saving his cameras began to wear off and he really felt his injuries for the first time. It turned out that he had a badly bruised hip and what seemed to be two or three cracked ribs, with a measure of shock thrown in, so it was clear enough that the walk to the lake was out of the question. We got back to the *Puma* as fast as we could and ran home, where we got him to bed with a good stiff drink and such other comforts as we could devise.

Agustin suggested a quiet afternoon for us all, fol-lowed by renewed exploration of the chalkstream in the evening. He was upset about Lee and anxious to call a doctor for him, but the nearest doctor, so far as we knew at that time, was in Osorno, and Lee was rest-ing comfortably so we decided to send the message from the hotel at Petrohue when we went down to fish in the evening.

It is difficult to write well of one's friends and difficult for me to describe now how warmly and naturally Lee and I had been fitted into Agustin's household; it was as though we had been there for years, not a day or two, and as though we were friends of a lifetime instead of chance travelers. Of Agustin's four children only the two younger ones were with him at that time—Robin, a slender fourteen-year-old who was about to leave for military school, and Marisol, a charming seventeen-year-old daughter who was as graceful a hostess as one is likely to know. Marisol's governess, Martha, Agustin's pilot, Gerry, an Austrian ski instructor, Sepp Molinger, and Agustin's eleven-year-old nephew, Edmundito, made up the household. Martha was Swiss, Gerry was German, Sepp Austrian, Lee American, myself Canadian and the Edwards were Chilean, but everyone spoke English, and English was the language we used for the most part.

We needed a common language, because we talked a lot. Both Robin and Marisol were astonishingly mature for their age and could contribute skillfully and delightfully to almost any subject that came up, from music to nationalism. Even Edmundito could find just the right words at times. Sepp, Gerry and Martha—Martha at intervals of her daily task of knitting a pair of gloves—had fascinating things to say of Europe, often from sharply different points of view. Everyone, it seemed, knew about music and there was much music in the house, in the small library, in phonograph records, in Agustin's new composition that was taking shape on the piano, a few notes at a time in intervals between each day's many activities.

I had known of Agustin before I met him that he was a great man in Chile, head of the Edwards family that had arrived there from England in the seventeenth century. I knew he was the publisher of *El Mercurio*, Chile's greatest newspaper, and head of Chile's greatest bank and active in an assortment of business enterprises from whaling to soap-making. I think I knew also that he had been captain of the Chilean ski team and I certainly knew he was a keen fisherman. But I was not prepared to find him also an artist of considerable talent, a practiced translator and a really gifted amateur of music. I learned from Gerry that he holds a commercial pilot's license and flies his own plane from Santiago to New York whenever he feels like it; from Sepp that he had designed and built the small speedboat that was used as an understudy to the *Puma;* and from my own observation that such a combination of knowledge and talent and skill can make a man an intensely rewarding companion.

The afternoon passed very quickly and when we looked in on Lee at five o'clock he was sleeping peacefully, so we decided to set out for the chalkstream. Sepp elected to come with us, and we walked down the hill to the little temporary wharf where the *Puma* was tied, balancing carefully with our gear along the planks. At the last moment Robin decided to join us and came running down the hill. Aboard the *Puma* he found he had forgotten his reel, so he jumped back to the wharf and hurried off to fetch it. Running along the planks he tripped and fell hard, gashing his head quite badly against a concrete block.

The cut was an ugly affair, welling blood, and might easily have been the outward and visible sign of a fractured skull. But Robin was calm and conscious, scolding himself for carelessness. He talked easily and cheerfully and I thought him far better than we had any reason to hope he would be, though it was obvious his scalp would need a few stitches. So Agustin went off to get word to the doctor while Martha and Marisol brought hot water and alcohol and penicillin powder from the house, so that I could clean the cut and bandage it. Then we got Robin into the oxcart and took him up the hill to the lodge, in spite of his protests.

Agustin came back very quickly, with news that a holidaying doctor was staying at Peulla, at the head of the lake, and Gerry was already on his way in the *Puma* to pick him up. Robin was fine, neither sleepy nor depressed. Lee woke up and said a Martini would go well before dinner. The doctor arrived and we all had Martinis. Both patients looked fine to him, though he confirmed Lee's cracked ribs and Robin's need of stitches. The doctor left soon after dinner and Agustin and I sat talking while we waited for Gerry to come back with the *Puma*. We talked children and education and music. At intervals we played phonograph records, from Bach to Britten, with Handel, Mozart, Monteverdi and Purcell whenever the talk led to them. We talked of similarities and differences in Chile and Canada, of young countries generally and American countries generally, and of the economic overdependence of young countries upon the United States. I thought this a passing phase for Canada, not necessarily injurious. Agustin wondered for Chile, though, like most Chileans, he is well disposed toward the United States. I suggested that American technological genius is like British genius in government; the test will be in whether they know when to move out and let the other guy run his own affairs. Then Gerry came safely back from the quiet lake and we all had a nightcap and went to bed.

I fished one more day on the Petrohue with Sepp Molinger, because Lee was not feeling well enough to go out. I chose to work the big rapid at the outlet of the lake, from the right bank this time instead of the rocky island, and found it just as good as the other side. The big rainbows took my fly in the white water until I had half a dozen three- and four-pounders on the bank and had missed as many more.

Then for some reason I went upstream, climbed on to a rock and cast across the smooth draw of current just above the break of the rapids. A big fish boiled behind the fly as it worked across. I threw again, kept the fly quiet and had him solidly. He was big and brown and very sulky about it all, but I held him and made him fight it out in the smooth water above the rapid until I had enough control to know I could keep him from running out into the center of the rapid and carrying my line around a rock. Netting him was something else. My net was too small to hold him, the shore was far too rough and rocky to offer any safety in beaching him and the rock on which I was standing was the last place in the world from which to try tricks like gilling him.

I shortened up all I dared, scrambled down from the

rock into the water, then let the fish go bouncing down among the rocks at the edge of the rapid, where I knew I could keep the line clear. I followed him and then, because he seemed thoroughly exhausted, had a second thought about the size of my net. I led him over it, got his head in, somehow grabbed fish and net tight against my waders and stumbled ashore. He weighed just under seven pounds, the biggest fish I had had from a Chilean stream, if he could be said to be from the stream and not the lake. He was a brown-gold fish and handsome, with a scattering of red spots, but I wondered if I should have made out so easily with a rainbow of the same size.

As we passed the little hotel we stopped for a farewell word and a drink with Pancho Jones. Pancho saw the big fish and said that it was what he had been calling a salmon, though smaller than most. I assured him it was a brown trout, but it is worth noting that the only fish I caught in Chile with signs of salt-water growth on their scales were from the Petrohue. This fish was not one of them, but three rainbows from the first rapid and four brown trout from the mouth of the chalkstream were.

I like to think I shall fish the Petrohue again, for a longer time and later in the season. Agustin wrote me that on March 31 of that same year, fishing the rapid below the outlet, he caught six rainbows and brown trout averaging six pounds and capped them with another brown trout weighing fourteen and a half pounds—a range of weights almost exactly double those in my catch of February 10, and a formidable string of trout in any man's hands.

Lee felt well enough to travel the next day and we were overdue in Argentina, so Marisol and Martha and Sepp and Edmundito ran us up in the *Puma* to Peulla and the start of the pass through the Andes. It was a rainy day, with clouds holding low over the lake, and a sad day. We got Lee to bed in the hotel to rest for the next day's journey, then went down and had tea to warm us. Marisol made a sketch of Edmundito and another of Martha as the market-woman of Peulla. After tea we walked through pouring rain to see the slender, wispy drop of the Cascada de los Novios among rock and ferns and dripping Chilean plants. Sepp, who was once a world's champion, stirred his voice to yodel. Martha called him a shepherd and he asked her what she was doing at the Bridegroom's Falls.

Ten or fifteen minutes later the *Puma* was disappearing down the misty lake, with Sepp and Martha and Edmundito waving and Marisol whistling through her fingers as Sepp had taught her. I turned away and was sad to be leaving Chile, even for a new country and more fishing.

Journey to Argentina

T HE SOUTHERN ROUTE FROM CHILE TO Argentina, by Perez Rosales Pass, is essentially a tourist way, a lovely journey of short roads and long lakes between the high peaks of the Cordillera at an elevation of no more than four thousand feet. The first part of this journey, as most tourists see it, is the bus ride from Puerto Varas to Petrohue and the trip up Todos Los Santos Lake to Peulla in the little steamer *Esmeralda*— a name repeatedly famous in Chilean naval history.

In Peulla, Lee and I boarded a very crowded bus at about nine o'clock in the morning following our arrival from Playa Venado and started up the steep climb to the pass. The road was narrow and none too good, and occasionally the buses had to stop and back up before they could make the hairpin bends. But the drivers took it all very much for granted and the crowded passengers never for a moment checked their vocal admiration of the scenery.

We had been through some minor Chilean immigration formalities at the hotel the night before and the stop at Casa Pangue, the Chilean border post manned by carabineros, seemed mainly designed to give everyone a chance to walk around and look up at the magnificent glaciers and formidable peaks of El Tronador, the supreme mountain of the pass and the whole general area. The border was somewhere just beyond Casa Pangue, but just where I was never quite sure, because the lively passengers kept identifying every fence line or gap between the trees as "La Frontera." But we passed it somewhere and two or three Argentine military types, carrying crops and wearing side arms, leaped aboard and rode downhill with us to a tiny hotel at Puerto Frias, where we struggled through some rather sour and unpleasant Argentine customs and immigration routines. Peron's shadow and his pictured profile were upon us; one does not get out from under either of them very easily in Argentina.

It was a lovely day, and no one was too much in-
sulted or inconvenienced, though a charming Mrs. Smith
from Wisconsin would keep forgetting her solemn prom-
ises to all of us not to say a kind or unkind word about
Señor Peron once the border was passed. Her instinc-
tive, or compulsive, exercises in free speech somehow
escaped notice and we all happily boarded a tiny lake
boat, which immediately pulled out and ran us down
Laguna Frias, among mountains so close and steep and
high that they seemed to overhang the little lake. At
the foot of the lake we boarded more buses and ran
quickly down through magnificent timber, with enormous specimens of beech and cedar, to Puerto Blest on
an arm of Nahuel Huapi Lake.

Here again there was a small hotel and this time, instead of immigration formalities, there was a very fair
lunch, served while we waited for the lake boat to
come in for us. The boat was late, so I wandered along
the shore of the lake to the mouth of Rio Frias, turning over rocks and looking for trout food. There was
plenty. I found May fly, sedge and midge larvae, a few
leeches, some crayfish. The temperature of the stream,
which was cloudy with silt, was 56° F; the lake water,
a lovely blue and perfectly clear, was 62° F at the surface. If there had been more time I should certainly
have put up a rod and tried things near the meeting of
temperatures, though no fish were showing. As it was
I borrowed a rowboat from someone and Mr. Smith
and I rowed out to make a plankton haul from seventy-
five feet and take a series of temperature readings.

We were still at it when the boat arrived, a large and
handsome motor vessel whose name I forget, reputed

to be the largest lake boat in South America. She was
crowded with sight-seeing passengers, some of whom
came ashore to pass through to Chile by the way we
had come. The boat still seemed crowded, but we
crammed ourselves aboard somehow and very soon she
pulled out on the run down the lake to Llao Llao and
San Carlos de Bariloche.

Nahuel Huapi is a very big lake, about sixty miles
long, generally narrow, with several large islands and
many arms that cut far back between the mountains;
and it is beautiful on a very grand scale indeed. Being
a mountain lake, at an elevation of two thousand feet
and very close to the continental divide, it is fed by
a multitude of small streams rather than by any single
major tributary. The streams come down to the lake
through short, timbered valleys, directly from the snow
banks and glaciers of the high peaks. Valley after valley opens up as one travels down the lake, and each
is a natural frame for the loveliness of live blue water,
gray rock and the white of summer snow against a
brilliant sky. I was in no special mood to marvel, that
day aboard the crowded boat, among the exclamations
of my fellows. I was concerned about the vagueness of
the arrangements I had made for fishing in Argentina,
and the limited time I had left to fish the places I
wanted to fish. I was worried, too, about Lee, though
he seemed much better than he had at Peulla the evening before. But the wonder of the lake and its mountains forced itself upon me again and again, and I knew
that it was a realization of perfection for anyone who
has a love of mountains and water.

Toward evening we came to a beautiful peninsula

and saw the rambling, red-roofed mass of the Hotel Llao Llao, backed by mountains and surrounded by the rolling green fairways of its golf course.

The hotel is a showplace, excessively luxurious, depressingly North American in character and organization; Lee told me it seemed almost a replica of the Canyon Hotel in Yellowstone Park. But it is as superbly situated as any building possibly can be and every window frames a different view of water, often on two levels, timbered hillsides and mountains, sometimes carrying to great depth and distance.

We were comfortable and dinner in the enormous, elegant dining room was excellent, though the North American dance orchestra was a disappointment and the people at the crowded tables seemed to me to be straining for enjoyment rather than enjoying themselves in the relaxed and natural way of the people I had seen in Chile. Later, in the small bar upstairs, things seemed easier and more friendly, but even so I went out after a while, into the night behind the hotel.

It was very beautiful there, under the dark trees, with the high moon and the Southern Cross over the mountains. There were lights in the little valley behind the hotel, and from them singing and laughter, shouts of "Vino, màs vino," then a lovely Italian voice, strong and gay, singing first Italian, then Chilean songs to a guitar. I saw a white shadow behind me in the moonlight and recognized the barman from the hotel.

"What's going on down there?" I asked him.

"That? Oh, that's Little Siberia."

"What is it? A night club of some kind?"

He laughed. "No. That's where the help lives."

"Sounds a lot brighter than the hotel," I suggested.

He considered the point solemnly, listening to the cheers and clapping at the end of a song, then the start of a new song. "Yes," he agreed. "It is very good. They are happy."

The Manso Chain

THE BUILD-UP OF PERON—AND AT THAT time of his wife, Evita—is a fascinating thing to watch in Argentina. I had noticed it first nearly two months earlier, on Christmas Eve in Buenos Aires. At the airport were the faces, the dual, colored pictures on every pillar and wall, reflected from mirror to mirror, following from room to room. All the way in from the airport were great white signs, lighted up at night, "Peron Achieves" alternating with "Evita Dignifies," each recounting some accomplishment of the dictator or of Eva's foundation.

In the center of the city, walking around, I found a long avenue, one of the main shopping streets, where only foot traffic was allowed. Along each side of the street iron pipes had been set into the sidewalk and these supported immense pictures, mainly photographic enlargements, glorifying Argentine nationalism and Peron. There were pictures of football teams and ski teams and other athletes, Peron at mass, Evita giving to the poor, Peron making a speech; pictures and posters of the new Argentina, new provinces, new resorts, new medical services, new schools—all attributed to Peron and Evita. Lettered signs made any point the pictures might have failed to make: "No more faked ballots," said one. "Tourism for everyone"; "The privileged class of Argentina is its children"; "Justice"; "The Constitution"; "Industry." All taken care of, you know by whom; if you don't, you only have to check.

The avenue seemed endless. I followed it for fifteen or twenty blocks between the posters and they still went on. Strolling crowds gazed up at them, matter-of-factly I thought. One man made a joke about Evita, looked quickly around, saw me and grinned. It was the only comment I heard.

Then I heard a woman's voice, full and rich and beautiful, superbly trained, coming over loud-speakers from somewhere. I turned toward it from the avenue of the posters and found it at last in a great square where a huge nativity scene was set among carved and painted saints on a brilliantly lighted stage. The square was packed with people, quietly listening to that lovely voice in simple Christmas songs. On one side of the stage was a board with a verse lettered on it, a verse from one of the gospels I supposed, until I saw the acknowledgment of source at the end—Peron.

So again on the blacktop highway from Llao Llao to

Bariloche I saw the great white letters, for no special reason at all, PERON. And on a roadmender's hut by the little Minero River, pictures of Peron and Evita. Pictures of them again under a shake-roof shelter in the deep forest near Traful. And in Nahuel Huapi Lake, not far from Bariloche, Peron's atomic project on an island. A barman in Bariloche told me a joke about that: "One day something will go wrong out there and it will blow up. Then we shall have a new sign: 'Peron achieves: Enlargement of Nahuel Huapi Lake.'"

But the jokes are never freely made; there is always the quick glance around or the shielding of the voice by the hand, and one senses how deeply this thing has gripped the land and its people. The ostentation and glorification are not absurd; they are carefully calculated to touch the imagination of the semi-literate mass of the people. And many of those people have been materially helped, at least for the time being, by the policy of subsidizing industry at the cost of the country's true agricultural wealth. It is a step toward closing the hideous gap between the very rich and the very poor, falsely conceived, perhaps, economically unsound, rooted in tyranny, corruption and lies, but so long overdue and so desperately needed that nothing, not even full economic collapse, is likely to undo it. Even those who hate Peron and despise the ruin he has brought upon the press, the law and every aspect of true freedom, fear the chaos they know must come with his fall.

To say that one is always deeply conscious of all this in Argentina would be wrong. People live under it and for the most part live normally. But it is never far away. It is a shadow that bears upon everything, just as the lightheartedness of Chile brightens everything in that country. Perhaps the two peoples were always different, even before the coming of Peron. Certainly there is a Chilean saying, with which many Argentinos agree: "Argentina is a very rich country, but a very unhappy one; Chile is a very poor country, but a very happy one."

Whatever I saw of Argentine officialdom within the country was pleasant and smooth enough. Lee and I made our routine visit to the police in Bariloche the day after we arrived at Llao Llao and were received with great courtesy and consideration. Buying fishing licenses was a pleasant and easy affair. When I went to visit the Superintendent of Parks he was kindness itself, told me everything I had to know and assured me I was to consider all his services at my disposal. He impressed me as an able and devoted man.

During the afternoon we visited the fish hatchery, where brown, rainbow and eastern brook trout and Sebago salmon are raised in some quantities. Señor de Plaza, the manager, was a quiet and modest man, completely wrapped up in his work. I was disappointed that Señora de Plaza was away, because so far as I know she is the only trained biologist working on the Salmonidae in South America, but her husband was able to give me some of her excellent papers.

Argentina has a magnificent system of National Parks, stretching for hundreds of miles along the Cordillera and including all the finest lakes. Most of our fishing was in or near the two largest parks, Lanin and Nahuel

Huapi, which together run north and south along the
Cordillera for at least three hundred miles.

Nahuel Huapi Lake itself produces some magnificent
fish, though catching them is mainly a matter of deep
trolling. The world's record landlocked salmon (*S. salar
Sebago*), a fish of thirty-six pounds, was caught there in
1936; the North American record, from Sebago Lake in
Maine, is twenty-two and a half pounds and dates back
to 1907. The best brown trout I heard of from Nahuel
Huapi was a fish of seventeen and a quarter pounds.
The record rainbow was just under thirty pounds, but
a fish of twenty-five pounds was caught in 1952 and
fish of six to ten pounds are common. I brought back
scales from a few of these big fish, but the growth is
so even through summer and winter that no checks are
detectable and the scales are, like those of Kootenay
Lake fish, pretty well impossible to read.

I had no special wish to break any trolling records
myself, but Peter Weill very kindly offered to take me
out in his launch one evening and I was delighted to
go. He and his son had caught a fish of thirteen pounds
and two nine-pounders the previous evening. We started
at about 6:00 P.M. on a strong but dying wind and ran
across the lake at a fine fifteen knots. Peter put me
ashore at the mouth of a small stream to see what I
could find with the fly, while he trolled the bay from
the cruiser.

My stream mouth was a promising place, a good flow
of clear, cold water entering the lake over a gravel
bar that was built up for a hundred feet or more out
into the bay. It was easy to imagine good fish habit-
ually lurking near the drop-off for what the stream

should bring them, and an occasional fifteen- or twenty-
pounder cruising in from the depths of the lake toward
evening; and just as easy, of course, to remember similarly favorable creek mouths where such things have
proved themselves—at the twentieth, or perhaps the fif-
tieth, time of testing.

Peter's cruiser trolled slowly up and down, well out
in the bay. The wind died still farther. I worked my
fly deep and shallow, back and forth across the run
from every angle I could create. Nothing moved to it.
I let it hang and drift out and drown, then recovered
with a lively beat of the rod top. On the second re-
covery there was a pull, solid enough to be from a
heavy fish. I worked the fly back to the same place
and recovered again, and again there was a pull. But
that was all. Nothing I could do would stir another
fish, and even as the lake flattened with the wind's dying I could see no sign of any fish, large or small, feeding near the surface.

The evening hour or two passed very quickly and
Peter was back with the boat to pick me up long before I was tired of trying and hoping. Trolling had
found them nothing more than my fly had found for
me, so it may have been an off evening. I think there
is a good chance, almost any evening, of finding a big
fish with the fly near most of the creeks that flow into
Nahuel Huapi, and there must be times, especially in
late fall and early spring, when some of the creek
mouths would produce great fishing. As nearly as I
could tell the possibilities are not tried out very thoroughly except off the mouth of the Nirihuau, below
Bariloche, and at the lake's outlet into Rio Limay. I

should like to work the mouths of such streams as the Pireco, the Machete and the Vinagre, and it could easily be done because good-sized launches are available at the hotel for about twenty dollars a day, and it should be easy enough to share the cost with a trolling party.

Apart from Nahuel Huapi, its loveliness and its chances of really big fish, the best fishing within easy reach of Llao Llao and Bariloche is probably along the Rio Manso and in the Cinco Lagos area. Lee and I had only time to spend one day there with Gustavo Schwed, the Chevrolet agent in Bariloche, but it was enough to show us that the Manso and its chain of lakes offers a wide variation of remarkably good fishing.

Gustavo was our close friend and guide in all we did from Bariloche. He is a big man, with a long brown face that is usually solemn and is made more so by big round spectacles; he talks softly and seldom. Whenever we saw him he was wearing high leather boots and white gaucho pants; a white shirt with a brown silk handkerchief knotted at the throat, and an old green corduroy coat with a large white handkerchief flopping out of the breast pocket. No one could have done more for us than Gustavo did and his gentleness was unfailing, even though he was annoyed with us for not arranging to spend more time with him. He is a most intensely enthusiastic fisherman.

To explore the Manso system we left Bariloche early one morning with Gustavo's aluminum boat on top of the car and an outboard in the trunk. The road climbs southward along Gutierrez Lake to the low divide, then drops to Lago Mascardi, a big U-shaped lake which receives the Upper Manso from the slopes of Mount Tronador.

Beyond Mascardi the road follows the Manso pretty closely and there are many places where one can practically step out of the car into good-looking pools. We did not fish on the way down, but kept on past Lago Hess to the road's end just above the Cascada Los Alerces, a fine rock canyon fall with good water above and below it. I fished and caught several strong little rainbows of about a pound and a half, but found nothing larger, though Gustavo said that in the best of the season the fish average two pounds, with plenty of three- and four-pounders. The stream, which is one of the few that cross the international boundary from Argentina into Chile, reaches salt water in the Fiordo de Reloncavi, a few miles south of Puerto Montt, and must by that time be a considerable river. It holds rainbow and brown trout, eastern brooks and Sebago salmon, though I believe the first two are the more common.

We went back to have lunch at Cinco Lagos hotel on Lago Hess. This small hotel is undoubtedly the best center from which to reach the whole Manso chain, and the people who run it are thoroughly interested in the fishing. They have boats on Lago Hess and means of reaching four other nearby lakes, Fonck, Roca, Felipe and Linco, all of which are good.

We were told that the fishing on Lago Hess had been very poor for some while, except in the late evenings; but I wanted to see the lake and take a plankton sample and Gustavo said there would be no good fishing anywhere else through the middle of the afternoon, so we hired a boat and went out.

The lake is small, not over two miles long, and nearly circular, but much of it is very shallow, with narrow channels winding among rich reedbeds and there is little doubt in my mind that it is a splendid producer. The temperature at this time was 64° at the surface and 61° at sixty feet, the greatest depth I could find in the lake; considerably too warm to expect good fly fishing in midafternoon of a still day. But even so I saw one or two good fish bulging the surface near the reeds and persuaded at least one to follow and come short at my fly.

I was a little more hopeful of the Manso just above the lake, even though it was only a degree or so cooler. There are some good runs and pools in the stream itself and a fine force of water at the drop-off. I searched them all thoroughly and could find only some beautifully marked little brown trout of about a pound. But I think it is safe to believe that in the cooler weather of late spring and early fall Lago Hess must yield fly fishing as good as that of the best Kamloops Lakes of British Columbia, and the reedy bays and channels of the lake would make some interesting problems. It is a lovely lake to be on, with the great blue-green glaciers of Los Moscos Mountain above it and the wealth of bird life the reedy shallows attract; we saw ashy-headed geese, two species of coots, Chilean waterhens and several ducks in the short time we were there.

I suggested to Gustavo that we might well give the lake another try in the hour or two before dark. But he said he thought Lago Los Moscos, farther up the river, might be better and it would give us a chance to try one or two pools in the river on the way.

This part of the Manso is lovely water, not too wide to cover with a fly, but wide enough to be interesting. Most of the pools I saw were fairly deep, between rocky shores and broken by boulders and rock ledges, but with a lively flow of water through them and sharp rapids between them. I hooked a good three-pound rainbow in one of them and soon after a fish of about the same size flashed at the fly but did not touch it. I tried him again, several times, and several times persuaded him to follow into an eddy where I could see him clearly, though he would not take. I am fairly certain he was a Sebago salmon and if I had known then what I learned in fishing the Traful River a few days later I believe I could have made him—and perhaps other fish in the Manso—take hold.

We came to Lago Los Moscos at about 7:00 or 7:30 P.M. and launched Gustavo's aluminum boat on a slow-flowing stretch of the river just below the lake. It was almost a slough really, connecting the main lake with a round, reed-fringed pothole of three or four acres. The water was glass still and no fish were showing at all, but I remembered the fish near the reeds at Lago Maihue and began casting a green nymph close against the edge of them. In ten minutes or so I rose the first fish, a rainbow of just over three pounds. Then one or two fish began to show, still right at the edge of the reeds. I rose another fish and lost him. A fish showed well out from the reeds, then another and another, in bulging rises that did not break the surface; I saw a big sedge struggling on the water well out from the boat and a fish rose and took him down. A few minutes later fish were rising everywhere through the pond and all up and down the quiet reach of the river.

It was too late for the cameras, so Lee and I both fished. It seemed to me that for over an hour one or other of us always had a fish on, and several times we both hooked fish together. They were nearly all strong, hard-running rainbows, so we lost a few and we certainly missed a fair number of rises; occasionally we lost time in putting small fish back. But by the time it was too dark to fish any more we had half a dozen three-pound rainbows, two three-pound brook trout and a slightly smaller brown trout in the boat. I caught the first of the brook trout just as Gustavo brought the boat within reach of the place where he had seen a ten-pounder a few weeks earlier; its slow, heavy take convinced me for a moment that I had found the monster and the thrill was almost as satisfying as the achievement would have been.

We landed in darkness, with fish still splashing all around us, and packed the boat up to the car. Gustavo produced a great hamper of sandwiches and fruit and a bottle of wine and we talked contentedly of a well-spent day.

Traful, Meliquina and the Sebagos

A RAILROAD LEAVES BARILOCHE ALONG the shore of Nahuel Huapi Lake, but its destination is Buenos Aires, a thousand miles away. Travel through the National Parks of Nahuel Huapi and Lanin is by road, fair gravel roads for the most part, and by taxi, which is a matter of bargaining and calculation; time is fairly cheap—the driver will happily wait over a day or two for a long trip—but mileage is fairly high. We bargained with a cheerful dark-faced bandit who agreed to take us to Traful for about fifteen dollars, and on from there to Meliquina for another twenty-five dollars.

The Traful was an exciting prospect. It has a reputation as the greatest landlocked salmon stream in South America, and we were to fish there with Dr. Edlef Hosmann, president of the Norysur Fishing Club of Argentina and himself a fine fisherman. I had met Tito Hosmann briefly in Buenos Aires and had found him a hearty companion. At the same time, I knew he was a very famous sportsman who had represented Argentina in both international sailing races and the tuna fishing competitions. I couldn't help wondering why he should have agreed so happily to take care of two wandering fishermen like Lee and myself—or rather, one wandering fisherman like myself, for he did not know at that time that Lee was with me.

The road to Traful follows closely along the banks of Rio Limay from the outlet of Nahuel Huapi Lake. It was a brilliant day, and the beauty of the river astonished me. It is of good size, broken by small islands, winding among dry brown hills. We saw it again and again, sometimes close at hand, sometimes far below us as the road twisted and climbed several hundred feet above the valley. Its color was always a dazzling blue, so clear and brilliant that the eye could scarcely absorb its richness; and the shape and surface of the flowing blue ruffled in the valley winds, paled over gravel bars, broke in rapids, swung in curves of infinite grace between banks often dotted with low green scrub. No one seemed to be fishing it at that time, and it is a big river to reach without a boat, but I am sure there must be good fish to be found there at the right season.

At Confluencia, about fifty miles from Bariloche, we turned up the Traful. At first, after the Limay, I thought it a disappointingly small stream, but as my senses adjusted I realized its size was almost ideal, a river that could be covered anywhere by good casting and crossed by wading at a few favorable places.

The country changed gradually from the dry open hills to beautiful rangeland with dark tree clumps scattered through it, occasional meadows near the river and higher mountains along each side of the valley, many with great expanses of white slab rock that looked like snowbanks, others with ramparts and castles and turrets of eroded lava. By the time we reached the foot of the lake the hills were almost solidly timbered, with a mix-

ture of hardwoods and evergreens. The lake itself was
big and windy and blue, blue in a dozen shades under
the sky and clouds and wind. We stopped at a magnificent view point, where a sheer cliff dropped over a
thousand feet to the edge of the lake, and looked far
up the wind-creased surface of the lake to the mountains at the head, and down to the river's lovely outlet
between the hills. The taxi driver tossed his hat over
the edge of the precipice and roared with laughter as
the wind swept it up, back over his head and into the
trees behind.

"You cannot kill yourself here," he said. "The wind
will always blow you back." But he was wrong about
that as, inevitably, we later heard. It has been done.

We found Tito Hosmann's little farm above the lake
very easily and Tito and his wife Adela welcomed us
both as though they had known us for twenty years.
"The cottage is all ready for you," Tito said. "It has
been waiting a week. Why have you been so long?"

I told him I had sent him a wire, as I had to Gustavo
and the Llao Llao hotel, days before leaving Petrohue.
Like the others, it had not arrived. "Don't worry," Tito
said. "It will come. It will go to Santiago and to Buenos
Aires, and from there to here. But it will come very
safely, perhaps in one week from now. Not less."

Tito is energetic and resourceful; essentially an easy-
going man in most ways, and full of good nature, he is
as determined as anyone I have ever met over things
he considers important. "We just fish harder," he said.
"Where shall we go tonight? It is too late to go to the
river. We can go up the lake; it will be no good, but
at least you will see it."

We went up along the lake in Tito's jeep and I saw that, like Nahuel Huapi, it has only small streams entering it, directly from the high hills. All the big lakes of that part of the Cordillera seem to have the same general pattern—heavy rain-forest, with hardwood timber and bamboo, at the head, gradually tapering off to scattered trees and open, grazing hills at the foot, carrying on to bare hills and finally the open country of the pampas. The little streams that flow into the lakes are cold—50-55° F. The lakes themselves are warm at the surface, usually over 60° F, and the streams flowing out are three or four degrees warmer; all this in February, which would be August in the northern hemisphere.

We fished the lake at the mouth of Arroyo Cataratos, a small clear stream which entered at 52° F. As Tito had promised, it was no good, though one big fish broke water well beyond reach of my fly and I kept working in the hope that he would come closer in. Some tourists—bloody turistas, Tito called them—trolling off the mouth of the stream did no better and others casting hardware from the shore had nothing to show for themselves. But Tito said that the creek mouths can be fairly good at times for both landlocked salmon and trout.

We had dinner at dark and afterward a wonderful long evening of talk. Lee drew upon his fund of questionable stories, which is quite unlimited so far as I know, and Tito matched him on level terms. And Tito was optimistic about the fishing. "Tomorrow it should be good. The fish will be working down from the lake. We will go to the Long Pool, which is nearly as far up as it is permitted. The first three miles below the lake, which used to be the best, are closed."

The next day was February 16, and I know I shall always remember it as a great fishing day, in spite of my errors of omission and commission. It was a clear day, with a hard wind down the lake and the valley. We drove in the jeep several miles, back along the way we had come the previous day, turned in at the great Estancia Primavera and asked permission to go through to the river. Tito drove the jeep hard along sandy tracks in the open, semi-desert country. We came to a creek, took out shovels and built rocks into a reasonable ford for the jeep, then jolted and slithered across it. Finally a high wire fence stopped that kind of progress and we walked half a mile among low thorn scrub to Tito's pool.

Tito had thigh boots, but he had doubts about crossing the river in them. He took them off, took his pants off, secured his shirt up around his chest, piled everything else on his shoulders and started across. He made it, quite comfortably. Lee and I, following him in breast waders, were even more comfortable.

The pool was perfect, a two-hundred-yard stretch of good current on a slight curve, with a sloping beach of coarse gravel on our side and a deep run of fast water on the far side. Tito left me there with Lee and his cameras and went to prospect a little farther up.

I will not live over that morning again here on the printed page, though I do so often enough in my idle moments. I decided, with the best logic I knew, to fish the squirreltail fly that had done well for me in Chile. The landlocked salmon, I understood, fed mainly on crayfish. Probably they would not be feeding much in the river, as they were dropping back toward their spawning, which would start a month or two later. But I supposed they would respond better to something they had known than to anything else.

I was almost right. The fish responded. Working slowly down the pool I rose and missed, or lightly hooked, six beautiful fish. Some I saw as they came up through the sunlit water, others I felt and saw as heavy boils under the surface. Each time I found, in my perversity, some reason to continue with the same fly. I wasn't striking right, I wasn't working the fly at the right speed, I wasn't reaching the fish properly—everything crossed my mind except the thought that I might not be using the right kind of fly. They were coming to it, trying to take it. It had to be the fault of something I was doing or not doing. As it turned out later I am pretty sure now that any fly I had with me would have been better than the bushy squirreltail.

When Tito came back at lunchtime I was thoroughly ashamed of myself. He had two nice fish of about six pounds, taken on a Black Ghost. "Small fish," he said. "Very small."

"You should have taken the Long Pool," I said. "I've ruined it now. I'm sorry."

"It is nothing," Tito said. "They will come again. You had the wrong fly. A streamer fly is best, always."

After lunch Tito took me up to the next pool above. There was a sharp little run of white water over gravel at the head, then a deep swirling pool curving under a high cut-bank on the far side. I had changed my fly for a slender streamer pattern on a 6x long hook. In the

white water at the head of the pool a bright little fish
of two or three pounds took firmly and ran well. I
beached him and released him, an indubitable Sebago
and my first; if he had done nothing else he had proved
to me that they are mortal and, like other fish, open to
complete deception by the movement of a few feathers
on a hook.

Tito had told me to work my fly fast, both with the
rod top and by stripping. From the deep blue water of
the body of the pool a big fish came up in full sunlight,
following the fast fly; he swirled at it and missed, swirled
again and missed again, staying right on top of the
water. I took the fly away and he was at once obviously
confused, turning back and forth to search for it. I
rolled it out easily, six feet upstream and a little beyond
him. He saw it in the air and began swimming for it
before it lit. I let it swing, without work, and he inter-
cepted perfectly. It was a strike no one could miss and
I set the hook firmly in the corner of his jaw, from about
twenty degrees downstream.

All this happened very quickly, a fisherman's delight
and a photographer's tragedy because Lee had exhausted
his film on the small fish and was reloading his camera.
The fish ran hard for the deep water of the far side,
near the tail of the pool, but he came back easily, almost
to my feet, and I began to wonder if he was ready for
beaching. Then he jumped clear out, almost under the
rod top, and ran again. He did this two or three times,
always fighting hardest when he was on a short line and
seemingly exhausted, but in the end I tailed him—a fish
of almost nine pounds, silvery, very slender and graceful,
lightly marked with jet-black spots on the gill-covers

and upper part of the body. I have caught fish of more spectacular coloring, fish that were impressive because of their deep and solid bodies, fish that had the lovely blue-green and silver contrasts of deep-water feeding still full upon them, but never a fish with such clean and lovely lines and such grace of shape.

Soon after that we went back to the Long Pool and Tito proved his point—that the fish would come again. They came, all through the windy afternoon, fish of eight, ten and twelve pounds. We killed only six fish between us, because that is the unwritten rule of Tito's club and the Estancia whose land we had crossed, but it would have been possible to kill twice the number. As Tito said, it was a big day, very big.

The day taught me one more lesson about Argentine Sebagos. All the fish I hooked through the afternoon, except one, and all those I saw Tito hook, fought in exactly the same way. They ran well, but not far, perhaps ten or twenty yards into the backing. They turned easily and came back easily, only to jump in shallow water and run again, never farther than the first time. I thought I understood them completely.

A good fish had shown once or twice near a brush pile on the far side of the stream. It was a hard place to reach across the downstream wind, but I called Lee to be ready with the camera because I was pretty sure the fish would come if I could show him the fly. I reached him and he came, almost as the fly lit at the limit of the cast, in a slashing rise that shot water high in the air. Behind me Lee said joyfully, "I got it."

The fish began to work slowly and heavily downstream, still near the surface, right over on the far side.

The backing was out at once because the cast had taken the last yard of fly line, but I wasn't worried about him. I was still well up the pool and Tito was fishing eighty or ninety yards below me. There was no sense in disturbing his fishing, so I held the fish as hard as I could and backed out of the water on to the beach.

But he still took line, not in a rush but slowly, sulkily, irresistibly. I decided to go down and then, as I started, Tito hooked a fish, so I changed my mind and tried to hold again. He still took line.

Tito had his fish quickly under control and inside the line mine was following, so in the end I went down and Tito lowered his rod and I stepped over it and began running.

"You shouldn't have tried to hold him," Tito said as I passed. "Don't let him out of the pool or he'll be gone for good."

I still wasn't really worried. I eased the strain as I ran and got well below the fish, then waded into the shallow tail of the pool to work him from still more directly below. I was sure he would swim up when he felt the new angle of the strain. Instead he came slowly down until he was holding in midstream ten or fifteen yards directly above me. I tried to lift him to the surface, to scare him and make him run upstream, but I couldn't stir him an inch, though I could see the loop of my leader. I slacked away and he still wouldn't move. I decided to wade up and scare him. I took two or three steps, splashing considerably. He turned, swam straight for my legs, swerved round me and was away over the shallows with a speed that made the leader sing against the water.

I scrambled back to the bank and ran as hard as I could, but he was on his way, with over half the backing out again.

The rapid below was a rough one, full of rocks and split by an island. I managed to steer him on my side of the island, but that was all. The current and the rocks between them caught the line, jammed it and let him break the leader.

I walked sadly back to Tito. "He was either foul-hooked or awful big," I said.

"Probably both," Tito said unsympathetically. "You shouldn't have tried to hold him."

"I never had a fish do that before, run right down past me out of the pool."

"These will," Tito said, "sometimes. In a bad place like this you mustn't let them get too far down."

I realized then that the Traful fish, unlike sea-grown steelhead and Atlantic salmon, are dropping *back* to their spawning. There is no reason why they should have the same reluctance to run downstream as their cousins.

The next day was fiercely stormy, with cold rain and gusty, gale-force winds, and the jeep broke an oil line, which delayed us considerably. But Tito was determined that I should see more good pools on the Traful. We saw a great deal of extremely beautiful water, fine deep pools under rock bluffs, long gravelly pools where it seemed fish should be lying as abundantly as they had been in the Long Pool the day before, pools with sub-merged rock ledges, pools with gracefully spreading shallows at the tail, every kind of pool in which migra-tory fish should lie. But we found only two or three small fish, all under five pounds. It seems likely that the

day was against us, though it may also have been that
the salmon had not yet worked down to these lower
pools in numbers.

I would cheerfully have stayed on to fish the Traful
for another week; it seemed to me that greased line fishing might have been a method well worth trying for
the Sebagos on a bright day, and it is altogether possible
they could be persuaded to come up for floating flies;
a pool like the Long Pool would have been ideal for
both attempts. But it was time to move on if the airline's
job was to be done.

Tito thought we should try Meliquina Lake next. He
would come with us and Adela would follow later with
the jeep and meet us at San Martín de los Andes. We
drove to Meliquina on a day of alternate rain and sunshine, past the swamps and bamboo thickets at the head
of Traful Lake, through the dark rain forest, over the
pass and down by the head of Lago Falkner. Tito had
come through that country first on horseback, thirty-
five years earlier and had picked out his little homestead.
"And now look at the country," he said. "Full of bloody
turistas who throw out tin cans and don't know enough
to slow down when they meet you on a narrow road."
We did meet two or three tourist cars that day, but Lee
and I cheered him up a little by telling him of the atroci-
ties committed in our own poor countries, where lakes
are dammed and rivers polluted and forests destroyed
without thought of anything or anyone beyond short-
term industrial profits.

The Club Norysur maintains a very comfortable refugio or lodge on Meliquina Lake, with a resident care-

taker, José Navas, who is an excellent fisherman and one of the best fly-tiers I met in South America.

Meliquina is a fine lake, less windy than the larger lakes like Traful and by all indications a very good producer. Its surface temperature was only 57-59° F while we were there, dropping to 49° at the hundred-foot level. José thought we would find some fishing in the "Aquarium," a shallow part of the lake where big rainbows cruise among the weedbeds and rise to a surface fly, or off the mouth of the Hermoso River, at the head of the lake, where there was a chance of Sebagos and brook trout as well as rainbows. Tito and I, since we like to stand on our feet and fish moving water, chose the river mouth without hesitation; I was influenced, too, by the thought that I had so far seen only two Argentine brook trout.

The Hermoso is a very small stream, but it manages to split itself between gravel bars into three or four separate mouths, each of which holds perceptible flow for a fair distance out into the lake. Perhaps because I was interested in them for the moment, I was particularly successful in catching brook trout. All except one were big fish, within an ounce or two on either side of four pounds, short and thick, quite highly colored and fairly near their spawning time—within a month or six weeks of it, I judged, and that agrees with de Plaza's estimate of April as the peak of spawning months for Argentine brook trout. Without exception these big fish took the fly very slowly, ran slowly and deeply though with considerable power, and gave in rather quickly and easily. Not one jumped or even thrashed on the surface. They were, in fact, extremely disappointing fish, though I found the slow heavy strike an exciting thing until I learned to recognize it for what it was. Unquestionably their poor performance was partly due to maturity, but they were notably inferior to brown trout and Sebagos, both of which are also fall spawners, and in no way comparable to the single two-pound rainbow I caught off the mouth of the Hermoso.

While I was busy with the brook trout Tito hooked a four and a half pound Sebago which ran a lot of line on the light French parabolic rod he was using and jumped grandly well out in the lake. Lee hooked a few brook trout and a small rainbow, and we had one more four-pound Sebago when it was time to go back to the refugio.

Two other fishermen, on their way back to Buenos Aires after a hard journey with a jeep and a small box trailer to Tierra del Fuego, were staying in the refugio. They had been over to the Aquarium and had a nice catch of four-pound rainbows on big English May flies. José Navas wanted us to go over there the next morning, but Tito wanted to try the outlet stream, Rio Meliquina. José said it would be no good. We went anyway and José was right. It is a lovely little stream, but it was much too low and warm at that time. I found one good rainbow of three and a half pounds by working farther downstream than Tito, but otherwise we caught only very small fish. This was an unusually hot, dry summer in Southern Chile and Argentina; in normal years it seems likely Sebagos run down from the lake to the Meliquina sometime in February, as they do to the Traful. With a little more water to draw the fish I can imagine the Meliquina would be a wonderful stream.

We had to leave Meliquina that afternoon for San Martín de los Andes, our last stop in Argentina. But it was another place where I would willingly have stayed on for a few more days, if only to fish the Aquarium and hook another Sebago off the mouth of the Hermoso.

Rivers of the Pampas

APPROACHED FROM THE SOUTH, SAN Martín de los Andes must be one of the loveliest little cities in the world. One sees it first from a considerable elevation, a pattern of green squares and red-roofed houses half hidden by lines of poplar trees, marked out by the road lines, filling the flat land above the curved sandy beach at the head of Lago Lacar. The lake, like the Manso chain, drains westward, through Chile by the lakes Pirehueico and Panguipulli to the Enco and the San Pedro. The hills around the city are almost solid with dark green timber.

We stayed in the city at the comfortable little Los Andes Hotel, whose owner, Guy Dawson, a friend of Tito and member of the Club Norysur, had promised to show us the fishing. Guy is a big, heavily boned Australian, usually dressed in riding breeches, polo boots and a dark blue beret. He probably carries a few more years than he would readily admit or I would care to pin on him, but he is one of the finest horsemen in Argentina and still jumps in championship company. Apart from horses, his garden and his grandchildren, Guy's greatest enthusiasms are probably his English Land Rover and fishing.

He drove us about fifty miles to the river Collon Cura the morning after we arrived at San Martín. The road climbed steeply at first, past the big army camp, up through the easy pass that is San Martín's main communication with the rest of Argentina. As soon as we were through the pass the country began to change. The hills became bare and brown again, much like the hills of Wyoming, and quickly opened up to leave wide ranges of gently rolling land between them. There were only great estancias marked by their lines of poplar trees to break the brown pampas. Land was measured in leagues, sheep by the hundred thousand. We saw the high white plumes of pampas grass streaming like silk in the wind. A group of Darwin's rheas, gray, ostrich-like wild birds of the open pampas, was feeding within fifty yards of the road; they did not move when we stopped the jeep and climbed out behind it, and Lee ran his camera until he was ready for them to move, then told us to show ourselves and stir them up.

The road had followed within sight of the Chimehuin River most of the way, but near the Estancia Chimehuin it climbed a steep, high ridge and dropped over into the valley of the Collon Cura, a little way below the junction of the two rivers. Guy swung the Land Rover off the road and started across the pampas. We passed a little swamp, stirring up flamingos, geese and ducks of several species. There was no sign of a track but Guy seemed to know exactly where he wanted to go. Even when we crossed a strip of swampy ground and a wet ditch the Land Rover did not hesitate and finally it slithered down a bank of loose gravel into the rocky riverbed.

The river was a wide rush of jeweled water between treeless banks under the high and brilliant sun. It was sparkling clear and unbelievably full in the dryness all about. For the moment, because it was so new to me, I felt it a strange place to come in search of fish.

"Where do we look for them?" I asked Guy.

"Almost anywhere," he said. "It's good here, it's good farther up, it's good farther down."

So I pulled on my waders and waded out into the rushing water. I let out line easily, searching the water near me as I have always been taught to do, gradually lengthening successive casts until I was throwing the line I wanted to handle. About then the first fish took, hard and fast, on the swing of the fly. He ran and jumped in the leaping water and I let him go as he would because there wasn't a hazard or holt within sight. He was bright on the water, a clean, silvery rainbow of just over two pounds.

The pool I was fishing was a long sweeping reach of fast current over a gravel bottom, probably four or five feet deep, growing gradually deeper over on the far side, beyond my farthest reach. I had only to wade well out in it and reach over with a fair cast to hook another fish, of identically the same size and shape and performance. And another, and another. Just below me Tito was doing the same thing, rolling out a lovely fly with his tiny rod and forward taper line. He tired of it first and went upstream to a deeper pool by a cut-bank to search for bigger fish. I stayed where I was and tried to

wade farther and reach farther in the hope that a bigger
fish would be in deeper water near the far bank.

Nothing came of it except more silvery two-pounders,
every one of them a worthy fish and nice exercise for
Lee's efforts to catch jumps in his camera lenses; but
the very numbers of them convinced me that I was not
likely to find anything much larger, at least in this par-
ticular pool, which seemed wide enough and long
enough to hold a thousand of them. Tito came back to
say that he had seen some fish that looked larger under
the cut-bank, but had not been able to move them. So
we decided to eat lunch in the limited shade under the
roof of the Land Rover.

After lunch I wandered downstream and found more
of the same thing, lovely fly water with never a problem
anywhere in it and fish of about two pounds everywhere
through it. I did find a brown trout of two and a half
pounds at the edge of a deep back eddy, and a rainbow
of the same size at the head of a strong run over a slanting gravel bar, but nothing larger. We took home fourteen fish that day, averaging rather over two pounds.
I have no record of how many we released, though I
have a note that they were all between one and two
pounds. There is no doubt there are larger fish in the
river—Guy and Tito said up to at least five or six
pounds—and we might have been able to move one or
two of them after sunset, but it was a long drive home
and we left with the sun still high.

That day was the start of a heat wave which Guy
and his family said was hotter than anything they had
known in the past twenty or thirty years. It was a good
heat, fresh and clean and dry, born of the sun and bril-

liant with light, but it can hardly have been favorable
to the fishing in those sparkling, shadeless streams. We
went the next day to the Chimehuin, at a point about
thirty miles from San Martín, starting in at a good deep
pool just below a short, rock-walled canyon.

There was a scattered hatch of May flies on the water
at first and a few fish were rising at the tail of the pool
and in the next long, still pool below. I decided to go
down and try them with a floating fly. The first two or
three fish I covered, at the tail of the pool, were small—
not over a pound and a half. But they responded well,
considering the brilliance of the sunlight and the fact
that the hatch was almost over. By the time I got to the
long pool fish were rising only occasionally at long intervals, and too often in places I could not cover without
some drag. But the floating fly persuaded two nice rainbows, each weighing two and a quarter pounds, and I
felt my morning was well spent.

An island split the river below the long pool and there
was a lively run of fast water on the far side of it. The
place looked so attractive that I waded across to it before lunch, not without difficulty, and tried it with a
wet fly. About halfway down the run, in water silvery
with sunlight, a three-pound brown trout took the fly
in a swirl of gold against silver. The color and light of
the fish and the place were so vivid and strong that they
have remained alive in me, subject to recall whenever I
wish.

The Chimehuin has a few patches of low thorn scrub
along it and plenty of pampas grass, but the only thing
that offered us shade at lunchtime was a big old apple
tree. There were two or three others nearby, but no

sign of a house or other building within miles, so I asked how they happened to be there.

"They are supposed to have been planted by Jesuit missionaries over three hundred years ago," Guy said. "I suppose it could be true. Certainly there was a Jesuit mission hereabouts at that time."

It was intensely hot and almost windless, so we made use of the apple tree's shade for quite a while. A few cattle stirred lazily among the thorn bushes and tyrant birds hunted flies and other creatures. Doves flew down to water, and across the river from us a family of wild geese sat in a line along the gravel. I heard bandurrias calling and watched a small flight of wigeon seek out a swamp hole in the open land behind us. It was a pleasant place to be and we were pleasant company, but later in the afternoon we defied the heat and went fishing again.

Tito had a remembered place, a fine broad stretch of water near some poplar trees, with great clumps of pampas grass along the banks, where he thought he might find a big fish. Lee stayed there with him, to record his casting. Guy took me on downstream to find some more pools. It was all lovely water and I found several rainbows of much the same size as we had been catching the day before on the Collon Cura, about seventeen inches long and weighing exactly two and a quarter pounds.

Early in the evening I was fishing a broad glassy pool on a curve. I caught a fish or two on wet fly at the head, then saw a fish rise well down the pool. He did not rise again and there was no detectable hatch of fly on the water, but Guy said he had never seen a fish caught on the dry fly—he had not been with us in the morning—so I decided to try it. I watched the pool closely as I changed my rigging, but there was still not a rise to be seen, so I started at the tail of the pool and searched it. A good rainbow of about two and a half pounds rose faithfully to the sixth or seventh cast and I hooked him solidly, to Guy's surprise and pleasure. He could have been the fish I had seen rise before; the fly was within a few feet of the place. But I decided to search the rest of the pool and at the tail of the glide below the rapid at the head the fly was taken quietly down. Again it was a faithful rise and the fish was solidly hooked, a brown trout of three and a half pounds. This time I was almost as surprised as Guy, and I began to wonder if I hadn't missed a lot of wonderful opportunities in other places.

When we got back to Tito he had found his big fish, a splendid brown trout of five pounds. He was pleased with it, Lee had some good pictures and I was glad to know at firsthand what that fine little river could produce.

We had one more day on the Chimehuin. Tito and Adela had to leave for Traful in the morning and Guy was busy so Lee and I took a taxi and a driver who knew the river and drove out to the Estancia Chimehuin, where we got permission to drive down to the water.

It was the hottest day of all, windless and cloudless, almost too hot for thought of movement. There had been poplars and willows and pines and fine hay meadows near the ranch house, but down on the river there were only low thorn bushes over which the taxi driver draped a piece of canvas to make some sort of shade. We caught a fish or two in the glittering water, then thought it worth trying to cool off with a few bottles of beer and wait out the height of the sun. But the extent of our shade was far too limited. In a little while I wandered off upstream with my dry-fly rod; at least, I could get my legs in the water.

It was a strange time. The heat seemed to make everything lazy and tame. Fat white-faced cattle stared at me without moving until I was within a few feet of them. I saw bronzewing ducks and South American wigeons and pintails and teal closer than I had ever seen them. The queltegues—teros, they are called on the Chimehuin—let me walk near enough to see the scarlet spurs on their wings before flapping lazily a few feet away. Around a pool of water in the river bed a hundred black vultures were clustered, caring only to rest and cool themselves. And the wild geese were everywhere, ashyheaded geese, upland geese and Andean geese, in families and flocks along the river, swimming on the pools, flying out to some favored pond in the meadows; I could even see their white bodies against the green wherever a spring broke out of the distant hillsides.

The river was quite lovely, nearly everywhere fast over cobble-sized rocks, but with plenty of good holding water for fish. I searched among the rocks and found, as I had on the two previous days, abundance of good trout food: May fly larvae of several kinds, sedge larvae, some of them very large, and the ubiquitous apancora.

There was a long flat pool ahead of me, shining like a mirror in the sunlight and without a break anywhere on the surface. When I came closer I saw there was a draw of deep water along my bank, which ran off into a branch of the main stream I had crossed lower down. It was a convenient place to drift a dry fly, so I made a cast. Before the fly had floated two or three feet it was taken in a fast, hard swirl. A moment later I was hooked in a long, slender rainbow whose jumping broke the glass surface of the pool to pieces. He weighed three pounds and was the only rainbow I caught in the pampas streams which looked as though it had spawned previously.

In spite of the fish I had caught with Guy the previous evening, I was very much surprised. It was one thing to stir up a fish or two that way in the cool of the evening, just before a probable hatch, quite another to stir one from the bottom of a deep pool in the middle of a scorching afternoon, when nothing in the river seemed to be moving. I searched the rest of the pool with thoroughness and enthusiasm, and moved not a single fish.

Lee joined me just as I finished and I told him about the fish. "I've got a hunch for that little side branch just below here," I said. "There looks to be a deep place just below where it runs off."

We walked back down there and the place was even better than I thought, a really deep, smooth run under a mud bank, narrow enough to be easily searched. I searched thoroughly, from the shallow water at the tail, and about two-thirds of the way up, in the middle of the strongest flow, the fly went down in a tiny, innocent-looking dimple. I tightened on it and found myself fighting a heavy, powerful fish, obviously a brown trout. He ran pretty much where he wanted at first, in short, hard rushes, and I was afraid he might find a root or even a lump of clay on the bottom that would let him make short work of my 3x leader. But I beached him in the end, a five and a half pound fish in perfect shape, gold-flanked and spotted with scarlet and black.

We explored a few more pools after that and caught a few more fish. We took off our clothes and went for a swim—at 61° the river felt like ice water in contrast with the heat of the day—and we drank more beer. When we came to the ranch house I suggested to the driver that we stop and take in some fish. He came back at once with a most formal invitation to come in. It was a big stone house, dark and cool and slowly dying in its lovely surroundings. A sharp-eyed, bearded old gentleman, once tall but now stooped and cramped with age, greeted us with a sweeping courtesy that made the house a palace and the little dark stone-floored room a hall of infinite dimensions. He talked with difficulty, in Spanish and German, but he wanted to know about our travels, our fishing, about the countries we came from and where we were going. A middle-aged, brown-faced woman came in with a huge tray on which were piled plums and glasses and bottles of home-brewed cider and beer. The old man introduced her as his sister-in-law and a younger girl who followed her as his niece, then set about filling our glasses. He was very proud of the big black plums, the annual crop of a tree that he had planted in a distant, vigorous youth before his seven sons were born. The women talked sharply and well, always helping the old man without seeming to. It was hard to leave there. They did not want us to go, and I felt they were lonely for people.

As we drove back toward San Martín, the driver said, "The old man has had very many women."

"Where are the seven sons?" I asked.

"I don't know," he said. "The old man's temper was very evil and they went away. Perhaps they will come back. Who knows?"

In spite of the heat we may have been lucky in the time we fished the pampas streams. Tito says that nearly always there are strong winds there, so strong that they are tiring and discouraging. It is easy to believe that, but I should want to fish there again if the chance came. Collon Cura and Chimehuin are great trout streams, but there are others of the same system, Alumine, Malleo, Quilquihue, Caleufu, to name only a few, that I should like to explore. And I believe that the biggest brown trout that swims in those streams will come up to a floating fly under the right conditions.

Journey by Lanin

THE CHOICE OF A RETURN ROUTE TO Chile was not altogether a simple matter. The general opinion was that the best way back was the way we had come. I was obstinate enough to want to go by a different way and I had made plans that would fit a different way, guiding myself by the maps I had and a faith that the lines on them really did represent existing roads. One possibility would have been to take a boat from San Martín down Lago Lacar, then the road journey by Lake Pirehueico and the Fuy River to Choshuenco and

Lake Panguipulli, and so out to the Chilean main line. But much of that also was a way I had been, and a long, uncertain way. I had a date to run the Liucura and Trancura again with Eleazar and I wanted Lee to turn his cameras loose on the rapids. So I chose to go by Mamuil Malal Pass, which leads by the volcano Lanin to the headwaters of the Trancura.

The first difficulty about this was that no one in San Martín seemed to know whether or not the road was passable; some people said yes, some said no, but no one could offer recent evidence either way. The local taxi drivers were unenthusiastic about the prospect, until one young fellow said that he thought he might go if the price was right and he could take a helper along, and if we could get the necessary permisso for his car to cross the frontier; it seemed he had heard from another driver who had made the trip a week or two earlier— with, it was claimed, one tire ruined and miscellaneous damage to the vehicle itself. I suggested that the ruined tire might not have been very new when it started out and our prospective driver agreed. He would like to make the trip, he said; he had never been that way. But there was the matter of the permisso. It would be impossible to get it in time.

I thought at first that he was stalling for an easy way out, but Guy Dawson told me he was quite right—there had to be official permission in writing for any car to leave the country, from no less a person than the Governor of the Province in Neuquen. Guy and Tito, with the help of Señor Pedro Torres, our driver, drew up a most formal and correct telegram to this distant gentleman, apologizing for hurrying him, but urgently requesting that the necessary permisso be granted to permit the eminent Canadian biologist and the equally eminent American photographer accompanying him to continue their work of national importance. Tito pointed out that he considered "biologist" was the most respectable and imposing occupation he could ascribe to me and that the word eminent was merely formal usage; I need not take it seriously.

The phrasing must have been right, because the Governor wired his permission, with courteous greetings, on the day before we were due to leave. I was surprised and delighted, until it appeared that we had to take the telegram to the local customs office to get the actual permisso and that the office was never open before 10:30 A.M. We were there, promptly at 10:30, and were grudgingly admitted by an old gentleman in carpet slippers, who seemed to feel that business at such an early hour was an affliction bordering on discourtesy. Once we were safely inside, the atmosphere improved. He and all his staff were fishermen, the Governor's telegram was in perfect order, they were delighted to be of help to us and wished us a safe and satisfying journey.

It remained only to go along to the house of Pedro Torres and seal our bargain in excellent Argentine pisco, which we did. Now that we had the permisso, Pedro was enthusiastic about the trip. It was important to start early, he said, so as to get through before the streams from the volcano began to run too hard under the afternoon sun, but that would be easy. The road on the Chilean side might be very bad, but his 1937 Oldsmobile was equal to all difficulties. Pedro was a young family man who lived in a neat little house with a stone-floored kitchen and a tiny backyard. His children's tricycles and other toys were scattered over the backyard and I was astonished at the quality and workmanship in them. They were not only far better than similar North American products, but vastly superior to any other product I saw with the "Industria Argentina" stamp on it.

We managed the early start next day and the Oldsmobile carried us handsomely until we were well past Junin de los Andes, and forty or fifty miles from San Martín. There, climbing a rocky road up the first steep ascent, Pedro decided to replenish the car's oil and water. He stopped the motor, climbed out, filled the radiator from a big glass jar, then poured a quart of oil into the crankcase. When he tried the starter, the motor was dead.

"It is nothing," Pedro told us. He jumped out again, raised the hood, tinkered for a few minutes, then came back to his seat and the motor started. But it was missing and we stopped again within three or four hundred yards on a curving slope that must have approached forty degrees.

Once more Pedro was calm and confident. "It is the gas," he said. "It will not take very long."

Lee looked out at the barren, rocky country under the hard sun. "Do you think he knows?" he asked.

I was wondering about that same point myself, but I said, "He seems to. And he's kept the old thing running a lot of years."

Pedro was thorough. He went over the gas line from tank to carburetor, then took the whole carburetor apart and cleaned it thoroughly. He got into the car and stepped on the starter. It ground away, but the car remained inert. Pedro shook his head solemnly. "It must be the ignition," he said, then got out and went to work again.

No one has a longer or more consistent record of failure with reluctant gas motors than I have, but even I know enough to look wise and say: "Gas or ignition. It's got to be one or the other." Then my troubles start, because I never know which of the two it is or which of the infinite neuroticisms the two are subject to has taken charge. I began to have serious doubts about Pedro, in spite of his air of efficiency and his enormous kit of tools. In fact the tools increased my doubts; to justify such a kit the Oldsmobile must have some formidable frailties; at the same time, if he did not know that the tools would conquer the frailties, why should he bother to carry them?

"Do you still think he knows?" Lee asked.

"I hope to hell he does," I said. "It's a long walk back to Junin."

Three or four vultures were soaring over the hill above us. "Look at those bastards," Lee said. "They always know."

Pedro was being just as thorough with the ignition system. After a while he said he had found the trouble, in the distributor head, and showed it to me. I could see what he meant, but I didn't suppose for a moment that the car would start when he had put it right.

A jeep came roaring up the slope and passed us with some angry racketing of the horn. Shortly behind it came a Ford, almost as ancient as the Oldsmobile, and behind that again a shiny 1951 Ford with a very pretty girl in the back. Both cars gave us to understand we were a blot on the landscape and an obstruction in the road, but neither offered to save us from the vultures. If it hadn't been for the pretty girl I might have thrown a rock at the new Ford.

"If this had happened ten miles farther on," I told Lee, "we could be fishing in the Malleo."

"And if it had happened in Pucon," he said, "we wouldn't care."

We couldn't have stopped at a much duller or much hotter place along the whole route. There were a few doves in the stunted thorn bushes, the vultures still wheeled above the hilltop, one or two hawks flew over. Otherwise nothing moved within sight of the road or of our short excursions from it. We had been stopped for two and a half hours when Pedro climbed back into the car and stepped on the starter. The motor ran. We congratulated Pedro, rejoiced with him, then piled in and got going again.

The road grew worse, rockier and steeper, but the Oldsmobile only climbed better and better. Soon we came upon the shiny Ford, stalled squarely in the middle of the road. Pedro managed to pull around it somehow, then we stopped and walked back. The driver said they had trouble, serious trouble, and could not go on; there was a noise under the car. I looked under and saw that the muffler was battered up and broken loose. Pedro got some tools and climbed under and freed it. We told them they could safely go on, then pulled out ahead of them.

"We should have stayed behind," Lee said, "and offered the girl a ride next time they're in trouble."

"Don't worry," I told him. "They'll catch up."

Pedro shook his head. "They will not pass us," he said confidently. "We shall have no more trouble."

We passed the older Ford, stopped by the side of the road and apparently waiting for its companion. The road was climbing very little now and we could see the Malleo River considerably below us. The twelve-thousand-foot mass of Lanin, white with snow and glaciers between its black, volcanic ridges and slides, was almost constantly in sight, and the Araucaria pines grew more and more closely along both sides of the road. I had never really admired the Araucaria before. Grown in Victorian gardens and on city lots as the Monkey Puzzle Tree it is a curiosity, usually out of place, seldom thriving, often sooty and dull. In its native surroundings, shaped by wind and climate, fresh with new growth, set off by clear blue skies and a mountain background, it is at once lovely and curious. We stopped for lunch among them, glad of the shade and the sight of the mountain and the sound of the swift river below, trying to learn from Pedro how to handle a goatskin wine bottle. Pedro himself was something of a virtuoso with it; he could hold the bottle a foot or so away from his mouth, tilt his head back and squirt a jet of wine down his throat; pressing gently with his hands he could maintain the jet at even flow and in accurate direction as he brought the bottle almost to his lips, then carried it away to the fullest extent of his arms. When we applauded he insisted that he was only a mediocre artist; there are many, he told us, who can empty a whole skin without slowing the jet and that in competition.

We did not stay long over lunch, in case the other

cars should catch up to us, but drove on to the little red-roofed Argentine customs house under the great shadow of Lanin. There was a considerable delay there, which I took to be disciplinary, because we were the only car in sight; then we were ushered into the presence of an army corporal. He asked a great number of questions, none of which seemed to have very special application to the matter in hand, then sent us back out to the car with a private who seemed to be in charge of the customs side of things.

Even the best of soldiers have no business at any international boundary, and these were by no means the best of soldiers. Lee offered our private a cigarette as we were walking back toward the car. He took one, then reached out, grabbed the pack and stuffed it into his pocket, grinning. When we reached the car he looked over the baggage, picked out the largest suitcase at the bottom of the pile and ordered it opened. Meanwhile Lee had wandered off a little way with his camera and started to take pictures.

I opened the suitcase for the little private and he probed around in it briefly, then noticed a rolled map lying on top. His eyes lighted. "Ah," he said. "Un mapa." It was a map of the whole of South America that the Parks Superintendent had given me. He studied it for some moments, then a window in the customs house was suddenly thrown open. A voice roared, "No pictures. Of the mountain, yes; of the little house, no."

Our private jumped, then fiercely told Lee to stop and bring his camera up. "He has not taken any pictures," I said, afraid for the film. "He was only preparing to."

Lee shut his camera away in his bag and the private seemed satisfied. He let my map roll itself up and threw it down on top of the suitcase.

"No," I said. "You will roll it properly. The way it was."

I had to tell him twice but he did it, and we were all good friends as we reloaded the baggage and he opened the gate and let us through.

It was a relief to be past them. As soon as I saw soldiers in charge I had worried about the power of the Governor's pass; military and civilian red tape usually make an evil mixture and it wasn't hard to imagine that some recent routine order calling for the use of a different rubber stamp might send us ignominiously back to San Martín. Pedro must have had similar ideas, because he was in great spirits as soon as we were through the gate, singing and kicking his vehicle along at an extravagant rate. Suddenly, at the top of a little rise, he slammed on the brakes and we stopped. About twenty feet ahead, at the bottom of a sharp slope, was a torrent of opaque gray water, with an equally steep slope leading out of it on the far side. The afternoon sun had done its work.

It was impossible to tell whether the creek was ten inches or ten feet deep, though the evidence was in favor of ten inches. Pedro eased down the slope and into it. Halfway across the motor stalled.

Pedro started up and rocked the car back and forth, but he couldn't get out. Finally he suggested that Lee and I should go ashore to lighten the load, which we did. The water was about eighteen inches deep, very cold and very fast indeed. Pedro, still in fine spirits, began the struggle to free his car. Somehow, very early in the proceedings, the horn stuck and sent its constant wail echoing around the hills above the roar of the creek. Pedro slammed and banged at it until he broke the window on his side of the car. The horn still wailed. Pedro roared his motor and suddenly the wheels gripped; the car backed up, almost on to dry land again, then roared forward, jolting and bouncing and swerving, hit the slope on our side and skidded its way up. Pedro tore the horn apart, stopped its sound and laughed in triumph.

A little farther on we crossed the real border, marked by a white stone Christ on a white stone cross, set among the Araucarias and against the mass of Lanin. We stopped there because it was a beautiful and wonderful thing to see in its loneliness, and Pedro was momentarily solemn. I fancy he gave thanks for the perils that were past and perhaps asked help for the others, unknown, ahead.

Beyond the border the road dropped sharply down to a little lake with a small logging settlement on it. A motor-driven scow ferried us to the foot of the lake and a narrow road that dropped still more steeply, following the Upper Trancura down to the Chilean customs at Curarrehue.

There seemed to be no one in the customs house, though the flag was flying bravely. Down at the edge of the stream we found two carabineros resting in the shade on their black ponchos. They jumped up when they saw us, full of apologies, and hurriedly put on their gleaming white tunics and buckled their belts.

Our business in immigration and customs was very

brief, but one of the carabineros was a collector of foreign coins; he proudly showed us coins from most of the South and Central American countries, so Lee and I dug out what we could in the way of American and Canadian nickels and dimes and quarters.

As we went out toward the car again, Lee asked the senior man, "Is it permitted to take a picture of the flag?"

"Of course," he said. "Of course."

"And of the little house?" I asked.

"Of course," they both repeated and carefully smoothed their tunics to pose in the picture.

Less than two hours later we were in the great hotel at Pucon, washing away the dust with hot baths and gin and tonic. We had been fourteen hours on the road to cover a hundred and fifteen miles, but none of it had seemed slow.

The Last River

I HAD CHOSEN TO COME BACK TO PUCON partly to fish with Eleazar again, partly to give Lee a chance to record the rapids, and also because I knew that Liucura and Trancura, coming straight from the mountains, would be considerably cooler than any of the streams below the lakes. Eleazar had warned me that February was a poor month for the Liucura, which is a very clear stream, but I thought the very low temperature would ensure us at least fair fishing.

To give Lee a chance of good light in the rapids we decided to work down only to the start of the heavy water the first day, then run the full distance to Villarica Lake the second day. Señor Rossello, the manager of the hotel, asked if he could come along with us to observe at first hand the complications of the fishing and judge what could be done to improve his arrangements, and that also fitted with an easy first day.

We started at Liucura bridge, as we had in January, and ran easily down to the mouth of the Carguello with very little to show for ourselves. There, in the great swirling pool where the two streams join, Señor Rossello, trolling a flatfish, hooked into a lovely five and a half pound rainbow. He had never fished in his life before, but under the careful instructions of Riffo, who was Lee's boatman, he did a remarkably fine job of handling the fish and made us all feel that the day was well started.

By lunchtime we had a few small fish for the pan and Señor Rossello's five-and-a-half-pounder. We had not even moved another fish worth keeping. I wasn't too disappointed; after all, we hadn't done so very well on the upper part of the river in January. But I asked Eleazar what he thought of the chances of the afternoon. He shook his head and pointed to the sky.

"It has been too hot, too bright, too clear for too many days. It is a very bad time." Riffo, the quiet man, nodded agreement.

"Where are the fish?" I asked.

Eleazar pointed to the tangle of drowned logs on the bottom of the pool we were standing by. "Down among the troncos," he said. "They will not move." And again Riffo nodded.

I still wasn't entirely discouraged. The Liucura was

52° F above the Carguello and the Carguello was an
even 50°. We would be fishing until well on in the
evening and I felt we were bound to pick up a few
worthwhile fish.

It was a wonderful lunch, with first-class wines—
Señor Rossello had seen to that—and Rossello himself
was good company, a round-faced, happy man who
loved to laugh. He was full of stories of hotel life in
every part of the world—he had served his apprentice-
ship in Paris, London and New York and built up experience in a dozen other places—and he was just as
full of ideas for improving the fishing arrangements from
Pucon. There would be a station wagon to replace the
Ford with no brakes; lunches would be better planned;
perhaps a small lodge on each of the upper rivers where
fishermen could stay overnight; some plan to reduce the
cost of getting both fishermen and boats to the water.
I hope his plans have worked out, but I should miss
the Ford with no brakes, and the oxcarts.

We were a long time over lunch and it was a pleasant, lazy place in a grassy meadow under high trees.
But I stirred myself in the end and fished as far downstream as I could wade, still without moving anything,
though the water was beautiful and I hung the fly deep
and long in a dozen good shady places.

And so, unbelievably, it went through the rest of the
day. We came all down that lovely river, fishing well
into the evening, without moving a single fish over fourteen inches, except Rossello's five-pounder. I had two
fourteen-inch fish in the boat when we landed and had
released half a dozen smaller ones during the afternoon.
Since I had never before counted fish under sixteen

inches, I could write it off as the first blank day of
the trip. And I had to admit once more that Eleazar
knew his rivers. As we bounced homeward in the Ford
over the furrows of a newly plowed field I asked him,
"What about tomorrow, in the rapids?"

"In Liucura, no good. In Trancura, yes."

The Ford bounced more fiercely than usual as we
came to another strip of plowed field and Rossello asked,
"Why doesn't he find a road somewhere?"

"He goes better where there is no road," Eleazar said.
"After all, he has no brakes."

Eleazar's forecast was accurate. We ran the rapids all
the way to where the river joined the Trancura without hooking a single good fish. The rapids were as good
as I had hoped they would be, full of sunshine and leaping water, and impressive enough for any camera. Many
places were even more difficult than they had been in
January because of lower water and once Eleazar, to
his intense disgust, wedged the boat against a rock in
a bad place. He wrenched it free without harm and
we both laughed, but I know how he felt and how
vividly the problems of saving gear and pride and dignity worked through his mind in the brief seconds of
suspension and effort.

The torrent ducks were still on their rocks in the
broken water; the cormorants were still around their
rookery, though they were fewer now and many of
the nests were empty. Just above the Trancura, Eleazar
pulled in to the rocky bank and told me to fish. Almost immediately I found a rainbow of two pounds and
another of three pounds, in little pockets of slack along
the edge of the white water. As soon as the second

fish was netted he signaled me to jump back into the boat, and we rode the big rapid down into the Martinez Pool.

The Trancura's difference was immediately apparent. It was not thick, or even milky, but the water had a gray-green cloudiness that at once swallowed up the transparent clearness of the Liucura. We caught fish all the way down the pool until it was time to stop for lunch near the tail.

For once in Chile lunch was not too peaceful. Fish were rising all over the pool and Eleazar wanted more of la mosca seca. So did I. I put up a small dark Wulff pattern that had done well in the pool before and waded out.

The first fish I covered, a nice rainbow, took well and came to the net without difficulty. After that I had several refusals and a few short rises. There was a vicious upstream wind and I was wading deep to reach the fish; then, too, rainbows are uncertain fish on a floating hatch, nearly always rising from a considerable depth and often swimming off to some other lie instead of staying in the same place to rise again. But I was pretty sure the trouble was not in these things, but in the fly I was using. The fly on the water was a small dark blue dun; a No. 15 iron blue would have been a fair imitation if I could have kept it floating in that water or if I had had any faith in rainbows responding properly to an artificial of that size in fast water. As it was, I found a fly in my box with a dark blue body and deerhair wings, tied on a No. 10 hook. As soon as I put it on my troubles about pattern were over. In quick succession I hooked three or four lovely fish, the largest of them well over three pounds. It seemed a good moment to stop for something to eat and a glass or two of wine.

During lunch we talked fishing and flies and rivers in the limited Spanish at our disposal. Eleazar was intensely curious about the other Chilean rivers I had fished, and especially about the Argentine rivers. Were they better than the Chilean? Were the fish better? Were there any good boatmen over there? We told him as much as we could and described the Sebago salmon and the eastern brook trout. He had himself been to some of the other Chilean rivers with other fishermen and one man wanted both him and Riffo to go to Argentina and run some of the rivers there. I suggested there might be difficulty in finding the type of boat he was used to. "We would take our own boats," he said, "on a truck."

No one bothered with a siesta that day. The trout were still rising in the pool and the hatch was still on. I caught another fish or two, then rapped the fly against my rod on a back cast. When I checked the hook it was broken. I had one more fly exactly like it in my box, put it on, caught two more good fish, then broke the hook in exactly the same way. After that I could find no fly that would fully satisfy the fish and in a little while the hatch ceased and the rise died with it. The experience matched one I have had many times in North America, when rainbow trout would rise freely to a much larger fly of the same general color as those on the water, yet turn away from almost anything else.

It was late when we left the pool and we had a long way to go to the lake, so there was not much time for fishing. But it was a wonderful afternoon. The river was low enough to force us to keep to the main channel and run all the big rapids above the ferry, instead of taking the easier water of the side channels as we had in January. Both boatmen paused several times to look over the water ahead, and occasionally, above some very fierce run, to consult. Riffo was always very serious and concerned; Eleazar was impatient and very quick in decision. Yet both men handled their boats beautifully, making every rock and eddy and twist of the channel serve them, never hesitating to run the full force of the stream through the wildest break of the current waves once they knew there was water enough to keep the boats from striking. Every so often it was possible to stop and fish for a while and we took a few more two- and three-pound rainbows, all the way down to the lake.

When we had landed the boats through the surf on the beach in front of the hotel, I felt suddenly sad that it was all over. I was tired in many ways. I had been living and eating and sleeping trout fishing, trying to understand new country and new people, for sixty days without a break. Yet I knew I might never see southern Chile or fish with Eleazar again. The next evening we would be passing through Temuco on the train, the morning after that we would be in Santiago. I stood near the bow of the boat, holding my gear and looking across the lake, toward the mouth of the river. Beside me, Eleazar said suddenly. "Tomorrow morning. The barra? At five o'clock."

The way he said it was between entreaty and command. I knew I should feel just as badly when we finished at the bar in the morning, but even a temporary reprieve was worth while. "Sure," I said. "I'll meet you here."

It was a still and lovely morning, almost dark when we started out. We were ahead of the other boats and Eleazar rowed steadily to make sure we kept ahead of them. He had told me many times how the big trout come up over the bar in the first light of early dawn and how sure he was that I could cast over them as they showed, without the movement of a boat to disturb them.

The main entrance of the Trancura was wide and smooth, black in the first light, disturbed by long, silent swells still running up the lake from the previous night's wind, lightly creased and whirled by the steady power of the current. Eleazar crossed the river flow well out in the lake, then rowed boldly yet softly up along the far side until we were inside the river mouth. Then he beached the boat without a sound and I stepped silently out into the water.

I saw the faint swell of a fish moving up close under the surface when I was still getting out line. I threw the big Campeone across, beyond him and ahead of him, saw the wave of his follow and the swirl of his take. I kept him as quiet as I could and held him as close as I could to our own side of the stream. Eleazar went well below me and netted him at the first opportunity, a four-pounder, clean and beautifully shaped. He brought the fish back to me and freed the fly. "It is a good morning," he said, his voice tense with excitement. "You will get six like this one."

I can't be sure he knew just how it would happen,

but he was right about the number. Within the next hour he netted five more fish for me, all three- and four-pounders. I lost two or three others, which threw the fly, and missed several that rose short or tempted me to strike too soon. Other boats came in, less silently than we had, yet fish showed behind them and took almost boldly until the light grew strong and the volcano stood clear against the sky.

Eleazar looked first at the sky, then at the water. "It is finished," he said, and I thought he meant we should go home. But he rowed a little upstream, then crossed over to the left bank and beached the boat. We left it there and walked for nearly a mile upstream along the gravel bars, crossing the side channels as we came to them, I in my leaky waders, Eleazar in his rope-soled alpargatas with his pants rolled above his knees. He pointed at last to a pool we had tried unsuccessfully to fish in the heavy wind of January. "For the big one," he said.

I smiled at that. "You won't catch a big one with me on the last morning," I told him. "I'm not a lucky fisherman."

Considering I hadn't been able to kill a five-pounder for him in several long and good fishing days, his reaction was surprising. He seemed genuinely shocked, as though I had blasphemed. "Not a lucky fisherman?" he repeated. "How can that be? They say you are a famous fisherman."

Perhaps my Spanish had made some misunderstanding. I'm not sure. But I tried to explain. "I never catch a big fish when it is expected. The best fishermen do. Perhaps I am lazy or I do not care enough."

He laughed at that and seemed relieved. I fished the pool and caught nothing. Eleazar searched through my box and made me change to an enormous white-winged coachman with a herl body a quarter of an inch thick —a fly I had had for years and never fished before. We wandered on downstream with it, talking a lot, struggling with Spanish words and extravagent gestures to bring ourselves fully alive to each other. He asked where I lived and how I lived and all about my family.

We were still talking when a good fish followed the big Coachman right into a tiny edge of quiet, shallow water between a fast run and a steep gravel bank. For a moment he was plainly there in the sunlight, his nose almost pressed against the fly. I moved the fly up a few inches, swung it a little over toward the fast water, then he grabbed it and went tearing down the run.

We talked on as I was playing him and when he finally came to the net we sat down and went on talking, because I saw that Eleazar was serious and very deeply concerned. I tried hard to understand. At first I thought he was telling me about his wife, who had died suddenly after they had been married for seven years. Then I understood that he had been married again, for several years, and was a happy man, except for one thing—he had had no child in either marriage.

Sitting there on the beach, under the new sun and the starting of the day's wind, we examined and tested and wrestled with his problem through the fogs of our different tongues. Eleazar had not given up hope. He was going to Santiago again at the end of the season, to learn what more he could from doctors and anyone else who might help. I searched for every tiny piece of knowledge I had that might strengthen his hope and struggled to pass it to him in the few words I could summon. I knew in my deepest being that he is too brave and fine and strong a man to be without children, and I tried somehow to tell him that.

Then he asked me again and again about my own family, one by one, their ages and sexes, their achievements in school or out. He was laughing and joking now, happy in the children as I was in describing them. Finally he slapped me on the shoulder. "Perhaps it is true," he said. "Perhaps it is true after all and you are not a lucky fisherman. A man cannot be lucky in everything."

We fished on down the river after that, but the end of my fishing in Chile was on that gravel beach beside the long run where we had caught the fish, talking the serious thing with Eleazar. It was the closest I had come to the heart of Chile, to a man of Chile, perhaps the closest I shall ever come to the heart of any man.

Appendix I. Tackle and Other Details

The intention of this book is to entertain rather than instruct, but I should be derelict in my duty if I left the reader without at least the opportunity of more specific information about tackle for South American fishing, and about the fish themselves.

I think I have made it clear that January and February are not the best months for trout fishing in Chile and Argentina, though they are ideal for weather. November and December are very good months on most streams, though the rivers are fairly high at that time and the fly-fisherman may find it difficult to get around on his feet. By March and early April the streams are still low and are cooling as fall comes on; these are the ideal fly fishing months, though one may run into bad weather, exactly as one may during September and early October in the Northern Hemisphere. But even in January and February, Chilean and Argentine trout fishing is wonderfully good by most standards and the combination of fishing and good weather is hard to resist.

The streams are generally quite large, and strong winds are common even in good weather. Besides this, anyone who fishes in Chile will at times—probably most times—want to use fairly large flies, as large as No. 4 and perhaps up to No. 1 or 1/0. For all these reasons it is well to take along the heaviest trout rod one can comfortably handle. The rod I found myself using most regularly was a ten-foot split-cane weighing seven ounces, though I also used single-handed rods varying from an 11-foot salmon rod down to an 8-foot Leonard. Most of my dry-fly fishing was done with an 8¾-foot rod weighing five ounces. Perhaps the most useful all around rod would be about 9½ feet, with plenty of power. Anything much less than this will not control a big fly in a hard wind.

At least a hundred yards of backing behind the fly line is a wise precaution. A four-pound rainbow in fast water will probably take about half of this on his first run, and such fish are an almost daily affair; a very much larger fish may happen to take hold at any time and if he does so in fast water a hundred yards may seem all too little, unless one is in a boat.

Large flies call for heavy leaders; 6/5 or 7/5 is not too much for a No. 1 hook. But there are plenty of times, especially in the midday sun of January and February, when fine gear is worth a trial. I fished 2x and 3x leaders quite frequently, though my usual preference was for 9/5 or ox.

Flies, as usual, can be a fairly large subject. I found the South American streams very rich in nearly all the usual trout-stream insects. May flies, stone flies, sedges, crane flies, deer flies and midges were abundant and varied in nearly every stream I checked, and the fish use them all at times, as well as land insects such as grasshoppers and beetles. From the evidence of cast cases on the rocks it is clear that the spring hatch of stone flies on some streams is enormous.

There has been little conscious local effort to imitate this natural abundance. Atlantic salmon flies, mainly

English and Scottish, are extremely popular, which is reasonable enough; they are nearly always effective for big trout. Some few of them, such as the Green Highlander and Blue Doctor, may be taken at times as imitations of natural insects. The Silver Doctor, another popular fly, is undoubtedly taken as an imitation of a small fish. The Black Doctor and Thunder and Lightning may represent apancora. Certainly all these flies catch fish.

A very popular pattern in some waters, the Norton, is probably a stone-fly imitation. I noticed it was usually spoken of as a spring fly and was most popular on those streams which showed evidence of big stone-fly hatches.

But when all this is said, it remains true that the favorite food of the South American trout is the crayfish, locally known as apancora. They were present in nearly all the hundreds of trout stomachs I examined, usually in large quantities. This crayfish is of the Parastacus family but for the practical purposes of a fisherman it is similar enough to Potamobius of the northern hemisphere. In the hard-shell stage they usually have dark olive green backs and very pale yellow-green undersides; in the soft-shell stage they are quite orange. The trout take them at all sizes from a quarter-inch up to three or four inches, though I think the most popular size was about an inch and a half with the tail tucked under. I am satisfied that the best imitations of these creatures that I used were the Squirreltail and the Campeone, both of which I have described elsewhere. I fished these flies on No. 1 and No. 1/0 hooks for the most part, though if I were to go to Chile again

I should certainly take flies winged with fox squirrel, in all sizes down to No. 6 or No. 8.

Streamer flies of several types do well in South America, and for good reason. There are always trout fry in the streams, as well as the bagre, a small catfish which is taken by the trout, fry of the pejerrey, a silversides, and of the perca trucha. I found the Gray Ghost and Black Ghost were quite commonly used, and I was able to do well at times with Iris streamers. Streamers seem to be far and away the best fly for the Argentine Sebagos, and one of the biggest brown trout I caught in Chile was full of pejerrey fry, though he took a Squirreltail.

Dry flies are best in fairly large sizes—8, 10 and 12— and with deerhair wings. Anything smaller is hard to see in the fast water, and feather-winged flies will not float long. Pattern is probably not too important, though I found flies of the Wulff-type generally very effective. Color is very important sometimes. Orange, pale yellow, gray and dark blue, usually with dark hair wings, seemed to be good. This, of course, is broadest generalization. There are places, such as the "chalkstream" on the Petrohue, where exact imitation of both imago and nymph may be very important, and I am sure there are major fly hatches of several types in Chile which I did not happen to see, though they may interest the fish very much.

I am quite sure that I rose at least three fish for every one I hooked during my whole stay in South America. Some of this may have been my fault; much of it, I am sure, was due to the warmth of the streams and the consistently bright weather conditions. But under nearly all conditions I met with I found the fish to be extremely light takers, and I suspect this has something to do with the manner in which the trout attack the crayfish. It is almost essential, for instance, to maintain a rod-top beat in working the fly; this has the effect of opening and closing the wings, especially in flies like Squirreltail and Campeone, and so of imitating the crayfish's quick, jerky method of propulsion and the opening and closing of his tail. If this movement is allowed to stop, most fish lose interest.

Even when it is maintained the strike is rarely hard and firm, except in fast and broken water. It is likely to be a series of very light plucks, as the fish follows around, and an attempt to set the hook then or failure to maintain the beat on the fly usually puts an end to the whole business. When I could maintain the fly's motion it was generally taken in the end, but very softly, so softly that the strike was seen on the line rather than felt, so I assume that the fish continued swimming upstream a little after taking. When I was able to handle this procedure in just the right way I usually hooked my fish, even in slack water. But I never found the fish easy and even in the very fastest water I often saw them follow the fly a long way before taking hold.

In spite of my errors and failures, I fully satisfied myself that the fly is at least as good a means of catching fish in South America as any other method. Jacko Edwards very kindly fished spoons and spinners and flatfish consistently as a control against my fly, and nearly all the other fishermen we met or fished with in a casual way were using hardware of one sort or the other. But every day I fished I had more fish of two pounds and upward than any hardware fisherman we saw and on all except two occasions—the Belgian gentleman's five-pound brown trout on the San Pedro and Señor Rossello's five and a half pound rainbow on the Liucura—I had the largest fish as well. I freely apologize for having been small enough to keep track of this point; my purpose was not to glorify myself, but to establish the effectiveness of the fly in comparison with other methods, and I knew of no other way to do it.

It is easy to become too much obsessed with the apancora and its imitation in Chile, and it pays to remember that the fish do take other things, such as insects and small fish. I often did well with much smaller flies than are generally used, especially in the middle of the day and in the afternoon, and I found the fish came to these more solidly and faithfully than to the Squirreltails and Campeones. In Argentina as a whole the "apancora take" was much less of a problem than in Chile, but the pampas streams averaged at least three or four degrees colder than the Chilean streams.

It is a serious mistake for the fly fisherman, or anyone else in Chile, to go hunting for monsters. Big fish are there, probably in fair abundance, but they are not caught every day of the week except in places like Maule Lake. Nor are they needed. No trout fisherman can reasonably ask for anything more than a daily run of two-, three- and four-pounders, with a constant chance of something a good deal bigger. This is exactly what most Chilean streams offer, even in January and February; to despise these and insist on monsters is to insist on disappointment. It is probable that Chilean streams once produced fish of a considerably larger average weight than they do now. But the fish are well established in most places, they have caught up to their feed supplies and leveled off to more normal averages. Any fish between five and ten pounds is something to be proud of. Trout of between ten and twenty pounds are memorable creatures in any country, including Chile.

I think I have said enough to show that Chilean boatmen are usually first-rate, both as rivermen and as fishermen. They appreciate a cheerful angler, who is willing to laugh and to try to talk their language. They appreciate, though they do not expect, a helpful fisherman. I fished a great deal from my feet—I managed to wear out two new pairs of waders in sixty days—but the majority of the fishermen work mainly from the boats. It is important to fish with a good deal of concentration, keeping life in the fly, holding it longest where it will do the most good, casting occasionally to places otherwise out of reach, watching always for the quiet, deceptive take of a fish. A good boatman will catch fish for a fisherman who does none of these things, but he will catch a lot more if he gets help.

Apart from the airline fare down there and back, which is between eight hundred and a thousand dollars, fishing in Chile is cheap. Hotel prices in the South run from three to six dollars a day, American plan. The cost of a boat and boatman varies from $1.60 to $5.00, though the average is about $2.50. Transportation of boats and fishermen to and from the river will add from $2.50 to $10.00 a day to this, though this cost can often be shared among several fishermen. I think it is safe to say that one can fish and travel in

luxury through the South for something well under fifteen dollars a day, and this cost could be held to about
ten dollars with care, especially if one happened to prefer the wading rivers. Five hundred dollars should cover
a month's good fishing and a look at the bright lights
of Santiago as well.

Appendix II. The Trout and Salmon of South America

All the trout and salmon of the Southern Hemisphere are exotics, from original plantings of northern fish. The first plantings were made in both Chile and Argentina in 1904 and the fish established themselves almost immediately. Some hatcheries are still maintained in both countries, but in most streams the fish more than look after themselves and I would judge that a fisherman's chance of catching a hatchery-bred fish is extremely remote. An exception might be the Lower Tolten, where a good deal of stocking was done after the volcanic eruption of 1949.

To the best of my knowledge and belief, only two trout are established in Chile: the rainbow (Salmo gairdneri gairdneri) and the brown trout (Salmo trutta trutta). The original rainbow stock was probably Shasta trout, from eggs stripped in German hatcheries, and the original brown trout stock was also introduced from Germany.

The rainbow trout spread a good deal more quickly through a watershed than do the browns, though many people in Chile believe that the browns tend to displace the rainbows later. If this does happen, it is because the feeding and breeding conditions of certain streams favor brown trout over rainbows, not because of predation by the brown trout.

Both trout have adjusted their spawning seasons, that

is to say, the brown trout has remained a fall spawner, though he now spawns in April-May-June; and the rainbow has remained a spring spawner, though spring months of the Southern Hemisphere are October-November-December.

I brought back from Chile about two hundred scale samples of rainbow and brown trout. Through the kindness of Dr. P. A. Larkin of the British Columbia Game Department, these scales were read for me at the University of British Columbia. The scales proved generally easy to read, with regular annual rhythms showing plainly, and rapid growth. All readings were made from scales mounted on blank slides and identified by code numbers, so the reader had no access to details of weight, length, sex or other information with the sample. Any reader is at something of a disadvantage when he has only a small number of samples from each river or lake, but this procedure, with the regularity of the scales themselves, does as much as can be done to ensure a high measure of accuracy in the readings.

Growth rates of Chilean rainbows compare with the best known from British Columbia; that is, those of Kamloops trout planted in barren lakes. Growth of brown trout was generally a little slower than that of rainbows, but the growth rate of both rainbow and brown trout was far less variable than that of British Columbia trout.

This strongly suggests that the Chilean waters have not become overstocked; the fish are still in good relation to their food supplies. All Chilean rivers I fished seem to have almost unlimited quantities of good spawning water, so it is evident that some highly effective controls must be at work. It seems likely that winter flooding through heavy rainfall is the most important factor. But predation by cormorants, black-backed gulls, herons and other water birds may be helpful in keeping the numbers down, as may the activities of the "native fishermen" who fish fairly steadily for food. On the positive side, the numbers and availability of the apancora are tremendous factors in maintaining a considerable stock of sizable fish. The apancora, constantly active among the rocks of the riverbed and highly predaceous, serves the useful purpose of collecting quantities of May fly, sedge, crane fly, midge and other larvae and presenting them to the trout in one large, economy-size package. Unless the trout become sufficiently numerous to make serious inroads on the breeding stock of apancora, there is every reason to believe the streams will maintain themselves at their present level of excellent fishing.

Many Chilean fishermen believe that at least some of the fish they catch are sea-run. From the scales this does not seem to be the case, except possibly in the Petrohue River, where the scales of a number of fish, both rainbows and browns, show a sudden, very rapid increase in growth in the second or third year. The Petrohue is a comparatively short river and it is the only river I fished in Chile that enters the sea at the head of a long, protected inlet; all the brown trout whose scales suggested salt-water growth were notably pale and silvery, while the scales of two or three larger fish, of typical brown trout coloring, did not have the suddenly increased growth that marks salt-water feeding. Altogether, it seems likely that a certain number

of Petrohue fish do go down to the sea, or at least to
the estuary, after their first or second year.

The Maule Lake fish showed the best growth of all
Chilean rainbows; a fish in its third year weighed five
and a half pounds, a six-pounder was in its fourth year,
having spawned as a three-year-old, a nine-pounder was
in its fifth year, having spawned at three and four.

The Laja River produced the best brown trout; fish
in their third year generally weighed between two and
three pounds; fish in their fourth year, between three
and five pounds; and none of them had spawned previously. A rainbow of four pounds was in her fifth
year, having spawned as a four-year-old.

I feel fairly certain that if other species of trout or
salmon than the rainbow or the brown had established
themselves in Chile I should have run across them or
across some supporting account of their presence. Attempts have been made to plant eastern brook trout
(Salvelinus fontinalis), Atlantic salmon (Salmon salar),
landlocked salmon (Salmo salar Sebago) as well as at
least three of the Pacific salmons, Chinook (Oncorhyn-
chus tschawytscha), Sockeye (O. nerka) and Coho (O.
Kisutch). If these had established they could be recognized almost by rumor, but I found no rumors. Genuine steelhead runs would also be recognizable; even if
the fish were winter run there would be the evidence
of the kelts at the start of the spring trout season, and
of the silvery downstream migrants. It is quite possible that the original plantings of these various species
failed because the watersheds selected for them were
not wisely chosen, though it is equally likely that salt-
water conditions proved unfavorable for the sea-going

species. In either event it will be a hard thing now to establish new species in the streams already well stocked with trout. I understand that landlocked salmon have been established in Lago Lacar, on the Argentine side, and I know that both landlocked salmon and eastern brook trout are present in the Manso system; both these systems drain westward, to the Chilean coast, so it seems more than likely that Chile will sooner or later gain these species, if they haven't crossed the border already.

One stream in northern Chile, the Lao, was stocked with fingerlings in 1950. In 1951 it produced five-pound fish, some of them mature; by 1952 it held fifteen-pounders. This stream was so saturated with nitrate salts that the fish had to be gradually adjusted to a similar concentration before they could be safely introduced, and it seems certain that their extraordinary growth is due in some way to the mineral content of the water. I understand they are breeding so rapidly that control is already a problem, but the almost incredible growth rate suggests that Chile may have a new means of stream improvement ready to hand.

Argentina has successfully established rainbows, brown trout, eastern brook trout and landlocked salmon. I have seen an unconfirmed report that sea-running Atlantic salmon are established somewhere in the extreme south. Efforts to establish Chinook, Sockeye and Coho salmon seem to have failed.

The big rainbows of Nahuel Huapi Lake make such rapid and even growth throughout the year that the few scale samples I had were impossible to read. Three-pound rainbows from the Manso system were in their fourth year, as was a fontinalis of the same size. But a number of maturing four-pound eastern brook trout from Meliquina Lake were all at the end of their third year, which represents very rapid growth. Big brown trout from the Chimehuin were three- and four-year-olds. It is safe to say that the same generally good balance that exists in the Chilean streams holds here too.

Señor de Plaza, of the hatchery at Bariloche, told me that he judged the peak spawning months in Argentina to be as follows: Rainbows, August-September; brown trout, June; brook trout, April; Sebago salmon, March. August-September would represent February-March in the Northern Hemisphere, which is an unusually early spawning period for rainbow, but which may account for the excellent condition of previously spawned fish. But I am sure it varies a great deal and that many rainbows in Chile and Argentina spawn much later.

The state of maturity of all brown trout I caught indicated May or June as likely spawning months. But all the brook trout I caught were going to spawn long before any Sebagos I saw. The brook trout in Meliquina Lake were certainly within a month or less of full development and I am sure would have spawned before the end of March. In contrast, gonads of the Traful Sebagos were less than half developed, and I do not think the fish could possibly have been in spawning condition before the end of April, if then.

The scales of all the Sebago salmon showed phenomenal growth after the second year, suggesting either migration to sea or a move of some kind toward more abundant feeding. The sea is an unlikely possibility since it would mean a journey of over six hundred miles, the last three hundred of them through the warm and very

TROUT AND SALMON OF S. AMERICA 281

muddy Rio Negro. A high proportion of the fish were maturing to spawn for the third time as five-year-olds, which makes such a migration still less likely. I think it is quite safe to assume that the landlocked habit has persisted and that the sharp change in growth rate after the second year is due either to a move from nursing stream to lake or to a change of feeding habit in the lake.

The superintendent of Nahuel Huapi National Park suggested to me that the Sebago salmon of the Traful had fallen off in condition during the previous few years. Tito Hosmann did not agree with this point of view and the fish seemed to me to be in beautiful condition, though slender. They were bright and firm-fleshed, with thick flanks and fairly wide backs, and they were, in every way, perfectly recovered from previous spawnings. Their slenderness seemed a matter of type rather than condition and it was by no means excessive: twenty-two-inch fish weighed four pounds or more, twenty-three-inch fish, five pounds; twenty-four-inch fish, over six pounds; twenty-six-inch fish, eight pounds; twenty-eight-inch fish, ten pounds. I have caught many a thirty-inch steelhead that weighed only ten or eleven pounds.

At the same time there is strong indication that the Sebagos and trout have severely cut into the population of native silversides, the small pejerreys, of most watersheds. The Sebagos may feel the loss of this forage fish more than do the trout and perhaps their average size will not be as great as it once was. But so long as fish of four pounds and over are recovering handsomely from second and third spawnings there can't be very much wrong with their food supply. If the pejerrey fry are no longer adequate, it seems that apancora is a very fine substitute.

There will probably be fluctuations in Chilean and Argentine trout and salmon fishing, just as there are in other places. But so long as the apancora remains abundant, these fluctuations should not be severe. It is quite clear that the fish are firmly established and that in most watersheds they have leveled off to a remarkably even growth rate after reducing the initial superabundance of the food supply. This level is an exceptionally high one for trout streams in any part of the world, enabling a fly fisherman to hold to averages varying between two and a half to three and a half pounds by reasonable selection. It is obvious that some control, or possibly a combination of controls, is operating to maintain this high level. It would pay both countries handsomely to investigate their fishing and determine the factors in the satisfactory balance between fish and food supply, if only so as to be in a position to prevent interference with them. Short of such interference the only likely hazard to the future of the fishing would be industrial or domestic pollution, excessive irrigation or excessive logging at the head waters, all of which can be prevented. It is fortunate that the best fishing is mainly in the upper reaches of the streams, where industry and settlement are light.

Reference:

Davidson, F. A., and Hutchinson, S. J.: *The Geographic Distribution and Environmental Limitations of the Pacific Salmon. U. S. Bureau of Fisheries Bulletin,* Vol. XLVIII, No. 26, 1938.

Appendix III. Some Birds of Southern Chile and Argentina

The birds one sees along the South American trout streams are a large part of the pleasure of being there. But it is hard to get good local information about them and almost as hard to get an adequate reference book. I did not find such a book until just before I left Chile and then it was obtained for me, with difficulty, from Buenos Aires. The second volume had only just been published. The title of this excellent book is *Las Aves de Chile*, by J. D. Goodall, A. W. Johnson and Dr. R. A. Philippi B.

Many familiar shore birds which nest in North America migrate to winter in Chile, between Arica and the Magellanes. One can safely recognize such waders as greater and lesser yellowlegs, stilt and spotted sandpipers, knots, phalaropes, curlews and several others. A few birds, such as the egret and the night heron, are practically identical with North American species, though presumably nonmigratory. A blue-winged teal was recorded at Ovalle, Chile, about four hundred miles north of Santiago in 1898, and the Cinnamon teal seems to travel regularly all the way south. But apart from these two the South American ducks are all different from our northern species, though several, such as the Chilean wigeon, the brown pintail, the ruddy duck and the various teals, are very similar.

Many other Chilean birds are obviously similar to,

283

but just as obviously not identical with, parallel North American species, and I found this evidence of long environmental separation wholly fascinating. Chilean woodpeckers and flickers, swallows, wrens, cormorants, sparrow hawks, redtails, water ousels and kingfishers immediately call to mind North American counterparts. It seemed particularly interesting to find that the two Chilean kingfishers are generically identical with the two North American kingfishers (Megaceryle and Chloroceryle), though specifically different; the scarlet breast of the Chilean belted kingfisher was a particularly dramatic surprise.

Many other birds that one commonly sees along the streams are completely different. The South American geese, for instance, are all shelgeese, far less impressive and graceful than our northern birds, but still very satisfying to see. The little parakeets were completely new birds to me, as were the torrent ducks, the magnificent great grebes, flamingos, ground tyrants, purple-breasted pigeons and many others. Those two familiars of every trout stream in Chile, the bandurria and the queltegue, were also strangers when I first saw them, though they will never be strange to me again.

Scientific names are generally a nuisance in the text of a book and so far as possible I have avoided them. But they are, in the last analysis, the only names with real meaning. The list that follows gives the Chilean name, the English name and the scientific name of each bird mentioned in the text, approximately in the order of its mention, and I hope it will be of some sort of value to fishermen who get the same pleasure from birds that I do.

BIRDS OF SOUTHERN CHILE MENTIONED IN TEXT

English Name	Chilean Name	Scientific Name
Chilean lapwing	Queltegue comun	Belonopterus chilensis
Blackfaced ibis	Bandurria comun	Theristicus caudatus Melanopis
Upland goose	Caiquen	Chloephaga picta
Brown pintail	Pato jergon grande	Anas georgica spinicauda
Bronzewing or spectacled duck	Pato anteojillo	Anas specularis
Magellanic snipe	Becasina comun	Capella paraguaiae magellanica
Rufous-backed ground tyrant	Colegial comun	Lessonia rufa rufa
Chilean flamingo	Flamenco comun	Phoenicopterus chilensis
Carrion hawk	Tiuque comun	Milvago chinango
White-tailed kite	Bailarin	Elanus leucurus
Sparrow hawk	Cernicalo comun	Falco Sparverius cinnamominus
Chilean tinamou	Perdiz comun	Nothoprocta perdicaria
Gray teal	Pato capuchino comun	Anas versicolor
Cinnamon teal	Pato colorado	Anas cyanoptera cyanoptera
Yellow-billed teal	Pato jergon chico	Anas flavirostris
Purple-breasted pigeon	Torcaza	Columba araucana
Chilean eared dove	Tortola comun	Zenaidura auriculata
Water ousel	Charrete comun	Cinclodes patagonicus chilensis
Chilean mockingbird	Tenca comun	Mimus thenca
Chilean parakeet	Loro tricaque	Cyanoliseus Patogunus byroni
Torrent duck	Pato corta-corrientes	Merganetta armata
Chilean eagle	Aquila	Geranoaftus melanoleucus australis
Bigua cormorant	Cuervo (cormoran) negro	Phalacrocorax olivaceus
Magellanic woodpecker	Carpintero negro	Ipocrantor magellanicus
Chilean flicker	Pitique comun	Colaptes pitius
Great grebe	Zambullidor huala	Aechmophorus major

[Continued on next page

BIRDS OF SOUTHERN CHILE MENTIONED IN TEXT
Continued

English Name	Chilean Name	Scientific Name
Southern ringed kingfisher	Martin pescador	Megaceryle torquata stellata
Night heron	Huairaro comun	Nycticorax nycticorax obscurus
Gray-headed goose	Canquen	Chloephaga poliocephala
Red-gartered coot	Tagua comun	Fulica armillata
White-winged coot	Tagua chica	Fulica leucoptera
Chilean little waterhen	Taquita comun	Porphyriops melanops crassirostris
Darwin's rhea	Avestruz de magellanes	Pterocnemia pinnata

References:

Scott, Peter: *Key to the Wildfowl of the World,* Severn Wildfowl Trust, Slimbridge, Glos., England, 1949.

Goodall, J. D., Johnson, A. W., Philippi B, R. A.: *Las Aves de Chile,* 2 vols. Buenos Aires, 1949-51.

Bennet, L. J.: *The Blue-winged Teal,* Collegiate Press, Ames, Iowa, 1938.

Kortright, F. H.: *The Ducks, Geese and Swans of North America,* American Wildlife Institute, Washington, D. C., 1943.

Appendix IV. Some Trees and Plants of Southern Chile

I am afraid I am an indifferent botanical observer and a completely inadequate botanist. There were many plants in Chile that I have been quite unable to identify, though they interested me greatly. There was the little flowering cactus at Maule Lake, for instance, and a splendid yellow lily that bloomed along the roadsides and in the fields, and something that I took to be a giant heuchra. I have still not identified the little scarlet vine flower that is *not* the Chilean national flower, copihue. I cannot even find proper names for the rauli tree or the Chilean bamboo. Nor did I ever learn the Chilean name for the giant gunnera. My sole justification for the following scrappy list is that it does touch some of the high points and may be of help to anyone who can find more adequate reference literature than I have been able to.

CHILEAN TREES

Chilean Name	English Name	Scientific Name
Ciprés	Chilean cedar	Libocedrus chilensis
Alerce	–	Fitzroya patagonica
Coihue	South American beech	Nothofagus dombeyi
Rauli	–	–
Araucaria	Monkey puzzle	Araucaria imbricator
Lenga	–	–
Maiten	–	–
Pellin or laurel	Laurel	Laurelia aromatica
Ulmo	Magnolia (?)	Drimys winteri (?)
Roble	–	–
Acacia	Acacia	Robinia (?)

The following trees have been imported and are thriving in many parts of central and southern Chile: eucalyptus, Lombardy poplar, Spanish chestnut, jacaranda, weeping willow, Pinus insignis.

FOUR SPECTACULAR CHILEAN PLANTS

Chilean Name	English Name	Scientific Name
La Bella Dormida	Fuchsia	Fuchsia macrostemma
Copihue	Chilean bellflower	Lapageria rosea
Colihue	Bamboo	—
—	Elephant ears, giant gunnera	Gunnera scabra chilensis

Reference:
Sudell, R.: *The New Illustrated Gardening Encyclopaedia*, Charles Scribner's Sons, New York, 1933.

United States Agency For International Development

La Paz, Bolivia

FROM THE DEPUTY DIRECTOR

Thursday, October 31, 1991
Acting Deputy Director Tate's Schedule

09:00	General Staff Meeting	(out)
11:30	Senior Staff Mtg	(in)
13:00	NAS Mtg	(out)
14:00	AD Mtg	(in)
15:00	DI Mtg	(out)
1700	DCM	out
